WOMAN

Studies in Critical Social Sciences Book Series

Haymarket Books is proud to be working with Brill Academic Publishers (www.brill.nl) to republish the *Studies in Critical Social Sciences* book series in paperback editions. This peer-reviewed book series offers insights into our current reality by exploring the content and consequences of power relationships under capitalism, and by considering the spaces of opposition and resistance to these changes that have been defining our new age. Our full catalog of *SCSS* volumes can be viewed at https://www.haymarketbooks .org/series_collections/4-studies-in-critical-social-sciences.

WOMAN

History and Critique of a Polemical Concept

PAOLA RUDAN

Haymarket Books
Chicago, IL

First published in 2023 by Brill Academic Publishers, The Netherlands
© 2023 Koninklijke Brill NV, Leiden, The Netherlands

Published in paperback in 2024 by
Haymarket Books
P.O. Box 180165
Chicago, IL 60618
773-583-7884
www.haymarketbooks.org

ISBN: 979-8-88890-318-6

Distributed to the trade in the US through Consortium Book Sales and
Distribution (www.cbsd.com) and internationally through Ingram Publisher
Services International (www.ingramcontent.com).

This book was published with the generous support of Lannan Foundation,
Wallace Action Fund, and the Marguerite Casey Foundation.

Special discounts are available for bulk purchases by organizations and
institutions. Please call 773-583-7884 or email info@haymarketbooks.org for more
information.

Cover design by Jamie Kerry and Ragina Johnson.

Printed in the United States.

Library of Congress Cataloging-in-Publication data is available.

Everybody knew what she was called, but nobody anywhere knew her name.

TONI MORRISON, *Beloved* (1987)

∵

Contents

Preface: a Fracture in History

"Ain't I a woman?" This question, which Sojourner Truth asked in 1851, has been and continues to be a source of inspiration and irritation for feminist political theory. Truth answered that she was a slave, thus breaking the unity of the abolitionist and suffragist movements from within, because she considered slavery a sexed experience and sexual difference a social experience. The black preacher claimed the emancipation of women and slaves, but in doing so she revealed the sex and color of the individual entitled to rights and the difference between those who *own* commodities and those who *are* commodities. Her discourse exposed a polemical line, because it invited women to join forces to overthrow masculine domination together; at the same time, she pointed out that the front-line of conflict was itself divided, because women were in materially different positions in relation to the social power conferred by skin color and property. The question "Ain't I a woman?" opens this book because – as the name of the woman who pronounced it while rejecting that of her master suggests – the answer is a *sojourner truth* that can only be sought in history. Thus, following the historical movement of the concept of woman does not mean talking about a sociological category, naming an identity based on anatomy or essentially feminine qualities, or representing a unitary subject indifferent to differences. Woman is instead a political concept that becomes so when women claim to define themselves against any manifestation of the domination that oppresses them.

As far as I know, there is only one work that already in its title explicitly promises to address the concept of woman. The author – Sister Mary Prudence Allen – analyses materials from antiquity to the beginning of the twenty-first century with the aim of affirming the "integral complementarity" between the sexes established by the doctrine of the Church. Allen argues that this complementarity is materially and symbolically rooted in the very act of the generation, in which the etymology of the category of gender should be traced. More than the history of a concept, Allen's is the history of an *a priori* idea that is constantly confirmed by the evolution of philosophical paradigms and by the thought of the men and women who practice them, whose deviations from a theologically justified order are accidental and ultimately irrelevant (Allen, 1997–2002). Despite aiming to give philosophical dignity to the concept of woman, Allen denies its political quality, which manifests itself when women refuse to be identified with their procreative capacity, chained to nature, and irreparably placed out of history.

This refusal leads to a subversion of the modern political canon, which has constructed its entire building on that identification. The works of Susan Moller Okin and Carole Pateman have shown unequivocally that the subjection of women, justified by their constant reduction to sexual beings, presides over the constitution of the sovereign individual and therefore of the state, citizenship, and democracy (Okin, 1979; Pateman 2003 [1980]). For this reason, when women contest the political and social position imposed on them by masculine domination, the concept of woman is charged with a polemical content that affects the origin and patriarchal semantics of modernity, thus revealing the irremediably partial character of modern universals.

Feminism inaugurated a historiographical revolution. This revolution is not so much manifested in the construction of a local and separate history, which women have practiced by collecting materials forgotten because they were considered insignificant, going so far as to coin the term *herstory* to name a narrative of events in which they are eventually protagonists. The feminist historiographical revolution manifests itself above all in the constant practice of a discourse capable of disrupting disciplinary canons from within, producing political theory by starting from the critique of historically given social relations and the categories that legitimize them   (Scott, 1986; Cappuccilli and Ferrari, 2016). As Wendy Brown has observed, this means that the feminist perspective cannot be confined to a "woman question". Rather, once it is recognized that women's identification with sex is the necessary and hidden supplement to the constitution of politics as a masculine prerogative, it becomes possible to transform a historically "marginal" position into the privileged perspective for understanding and criticizing the historical configuration of power relations (Brown, 1988). Under the impetus of feminism, the social production of sexual difference and its conceptualization acquire an undisputed political centrality.

The history of political and social concepts must therefore also come to terms with the feminist perspective, even though according to its highest theoretician, Reinhart Koselleck, woman is not a political concept. For him, in fact, the couple "men and women" is not among the "asymmetric counter-concepts" that constitute the "indicators and factors" of "a unity of political and social agency". Between men and women there is neither asymmetry nor antithesis, but mutual recognition, because the terms embrace the whole of humanity, describing its natural (i.e., devoid of history) articulation. After having defined the temporality of the modern era and its orientation towards the future with reference to the tension between the "space of experience" and the "horizon of expectation" (Koselleck, 2004 [1979]: 178 ff, 255 ff), Koselleck then speaks of "generativity" to indicate the transcendental anthropological condition of the thinkability of history. The relationship between man and woman is relevant for him only because it defines the "natural sexuality from which procreation springs", the "pre-existing zoological datum" which, by giving life to generations as a "generally human reality", makes possible the continuity in time beyond the limits of the single existential finitude (Koselleck, 1987). With just a few lines, Koselleck dismisses a fundamental part of the social history condensed into modern political concepts that he aims to account for. He erases the political presence of women who have spoken out from within the *Sattelzeit*, the threshold that opens political modernity. Finally, Koselleck denies women's action in history even when he speaks of the generational revolt of the 1960s in which they were collectively protagonists. This work of erasure is the symptom of a passion for unity by virtue of which it is inconceivable that the friend/enemy front – defined historically by the antithetical couples Greek/barbarians, Christian/pagan, human/non-human – should be broken down by the division practiced by women. Koselleck's passion for unity is therefore a manifestation of the patriarchal strategy that invokes nature to decree women's political indifference. To put it in Nicole Loraux's words, the "forgetting" of that division is precisely what constitutes "the political" (Loraux, 2006 [1997]: 16 ff) and therefore imposes the redefinition of the Schmittian concept at its root. For Carl Schmitt, the political is the "synthetic name of the origin" of a modern politics conceived as a "compulsion to order". In short, it is the exception that founds the norm and the contingency that establishes its necessity (Schmitt 2007, [1932]).[1] In contrast, the feminist perspective brings to light the persistent antithesis that, however hidden, prevents the constitution of politics as a unity, and cannot be resolved by a sovereign decision. The problem, therefore, is not to replace the sovereign decision with the "symbolic cut" made by women, conceiving it as the foundation of a "feminine" order different from the "masculine" one.[2] Rather, the aim is that of thinking politics by starting from the moments when women activate that antithesis and dislodge it from its forgetting. What makes woman a political concept – placing it in history and opening the experiences whose meaning it condenses to transformation – are precisely the women who, through their presence, their collective actions, and their speech, prevent the term from being occupied once and for all by the definition imposed by men.

The contestation of the patriarchal strategy exemplified by Koselleck's discourse has remote roots and the genealogy of women who practically questioned the consistency of the discourse that condemned them to intellectual,

---

1   Galli 2001: 733 ff.
2   On this conception, see Dominijanni, 1995.

political, and social irrelevance can be traced back to antiquity. The further
we move back in time, however, the more difficult it becomes to trace their
words and history, except for those handed down indirectly by men and then
collected in their galleries of famous women, aimed at praising the exception-
ality of some to confirm the rule of the inferiority of all. The choice made in
this book to begin with the early modern age, however, does not depend on
the scarcity of earlier sources, but on the idea that it is necessary to make visible both the hand-to-hand combat women took up with modern political discourse, starting from its incubation and first theoretical affirmation, as well
as the fracture that opens up in history with the emergence of feminism as a
political and social movement in the wake of the French Revolution.

Prior to this historical threshold, women who dare to write and dissemi-
nate their work in order to question the natural foundation of their subordination are first of all forced to justify their speaking out against the principles of
authority in force which condemn them to silence. Their authorial strategies
are singular antagonistic acts whose most immediate effect is to de-naturalize
nature and therefore to question whether being born in a woman's body has
unavoidable moral, intellectual, and political consequences. Their struggle to
define autonomously who women are thus makes the artificial character of
masculine domination manifest long before modern political discourse affirms
a conception of politics as human construction once and for all.

Whether it is thought of as a set of practical possibilities, as a substance
whose movement is manifested in the changing relationship between the different parts of the whole, or as a fundamental principle of spiritual equality in
front of God,[3] for these women nature is itself a historical fact and therefore is
not configured as a closed and unchangeable order, but as the field of a struggle whose stake is their freedom. The authors who wrote before the French
Revolution took advantage of the unexpected public presence of women during unstable and tumultuous historical passages such as the Western Schism,
the civil wars of religion, or the Glorious Revolution. However, they remain
eccentric singularities which, by opening cracks in the patriarchal order, move
on the threshold of a new order without the concrete possibility of shaking the
foundations of masculine domination. Before 1789, woman is the name of a
condition and a position that some women try to change, but it is not yet part
of an overall political and social semantics.

The fracture opens when woman becomes a "collective singular" that
expresses a claim for liberation shared by women who are in materially

---

3 See chapter 1.

different positions in society. However, the politicization of the concept of woman does not have the effect of unifying numerous experiences, in the sense that Koselleck holds about the "collective singular" (Koselleck, 2004 [1979]: 33 ff). Rather, in the very moment in which it opens a polemical front in society, the concept of woman is also internally put under tension by the multiple experiences of women from whose speaking out it draws its meaning. From the French Revolution onwards, women who think and criticize their condition – from a tribune, in the squares, in a room of their own – have behind them not only the multitude of women from lower classes who armed themselves to make the revolution, but also a mass of women who, from different positions, embracing the idea of equality, act against the patriarchal injunction to remain submissive in every political and social space. To speak of feminism as a movement, therefore, does not mean to look for the date of birth of the first organizations claiming this name, but to recognize the radical transformation triggered by the collective presence of women, which gives an unexpected political force to those who singularly spoke out in the name of a 'we'. Recognizing themselves as a collective subject and claiming to define their position autonomously, women therefore contribute decisively to the acceleration of historical time that characterizes the modern era.

The concept of woman is constituted in the tension between the experience imposed by patriarchal tradition and an expectation that rises in the face of the revolutionary promise of equality and freedom. At that juncture, feminist discourse is charged with a confidence in progress that constantly clashes with the different and subordinate nature of women that patriarchalism never ceases to invoke in order to deny them access to citizenship, even when citizenship derives its universality from rights declared to be rooted in nature itself. The trans-epochal continuity of patriarchy and the recursiveness of its arguments – which led Juliet Mitchell to define it as an "ideological atemporal" (Mitchell, 1966: 172) – make it necessary to rethink modern political temporality as such. If, in fact, as Koselleck believes, "progress" is the first category in which a determination of time unrelated to nature is condensed, the patriarchal appeal to feminine nature reveals the continuous presence of an 'anachronism' in support of the masculine politics of progress. As a constitutional factor of modern politics, patriarchy is this anachronism, which can under no circumstances be reduced to a backwardness of progressive history because it is an intrinsic necessity that persists until our global present. Even if it cannot be codified according to the modern categories of the political, because women are neither an external enemy or an internal foe, their ever-present and always silent subjection is what allows men to fraternize in order to manage power. In the concept of woman, demands for domination and claims for liberation clash, and this is why the battle of women to determine its meaning opens a fracture that breaks the homogeneity of historical time, making it an object of contention.

Contemporary feminist theory has polemically come to terms with the emergence of woman as a singular collective, denouncing in different ways and on several occasions the impossibility of unitary representation or universalization of a condition inevitably furrowed by multiple differences. The very possibility of defining patriarchy as an ideological, social, or symbolic invariant has been the subject of dispute, because it is considered the prerequisite for the construction of an identity of all women in oppression which is only possible through the cancellation of any difference determined by the color line, class, or sexual orientation. The most relevant outcome of this clash within feminism was to declare the need to abandon the reference to woman in order not to confirm the "binary matrix" which, by discursively producing the sexual difference between men and women, immobilizes the two figures in their natural determination and does not allow the recognition of subjective movements acting outside and against this normative dichotomy. The centrality acquired by the category of "gender" between the 1970s and 1980s is the result of this criticism. The category of gender does not simply rest on the distinction between nature and culture which – in Gayle Rubin's perspective – would make it possible to disavow women's identification with sex and therefore patriarchal "biological determinism" (Rubin, 1997 [1975]). Rather, it goes so far as to deny consistency to the sexed body to the point that, for Judith Butler, sex was "always already gender" – just a blank page, in itself indifferent, on which power is inscribed (Butler, 2010 [1990]: 9–10).

In the face of such a theoretical and political turning point, the centrality that this book grants to the concept of woman probably makes it "untimely": not so much out of time, but rather critical, in the sense that Nietzsche (an acclaimed misogynist that some feminists have been able to use against misogyny) attributes to the term. As Toril Moi has effectively shown, whether it is opposed to sex – whose cultural interpretation it would express – or it dismisses the category of sex by recognizing the exclusive centrality of the discursive construction of what is "masculine" or "feminine", the category of gender runs the risk of re-naturalizing nature, of de-historicizing the body and thus ultimately confirming the assumptions of the biological determinism it claims to challenge (Moi, 2008 [1999]). Consequently, while the extensive use of the category of gender by the human sciences ends up depriving it – as happened in the 1970s with that of "sexuality" – of any "virtue of division" (Foucault, 1977), the past and present insurgency of women as women is silenced again as an expression of a guilty essentialist identification between sex and the political and social identity, or of an evolutionary delay compared to a discourse eventually free from the use of normative categories. Treating the concept of woman as a "collective singular", this book instead identifies some moments of that insurgency, avoiding falling back into the essentialist guilt through a constant work of historicization. As Denise Riley has observed, whether declined in the singular or plural, the term woman remains central to feminist political discourse. To claim it without affirming an alleged ontological consistency therefore requires us to continuously think about the social and political process that from time to time produces it, the position of those who use it, and the political meaning of its enunciation (Riley, 1995 [1988]: 1 ff).

Moreover, considering sexual difference as an effect of discourse, and of the discursive power to normatively impose the distinction between man and woman, ends up treating all genders as equivalent in the face of power, or it leads to considering heterosexuality – the discursive and phenomenal coincidence between anatomical sex, gender, and sexual orientation – as the constant confirmation of the normative order that oppresses or fails to recognize those who, with their behaviors and sexual practices, do not conform to the binary matrix. This perspective does not allow us to consider the way in which the discourse that establishes sexual difference "takes hold" of bodies by placing them in different and not at all equivalent positions within society. The problem is not to attribute to the body a pre-discursive autonomous meaning or value, but to recognize the "sexed principle" of division of society that materially positions men and women within hierarchical and asymmetrical social relations of power, which constitutes itself as the matrix and signifier of any relationship of domination and subordination and which cannot simply be dismissed as a garment that covers bodies, because it is literally "embodied". To accord epistemological and political centrality to the concept of woman therefore allows us to treat masculine domination as a fundamental societal operator which, at the same time as it transforms the bodily fact of sex into a natural principle, symbolically enhances it by making it the criterion that structures the organization of society as a whole (Bourdieu, 2001 [1998]: 11).

Treating the concept of woman as a collective singular in a materialistic way does not serve either to identify the universal subject or to fix the homogeneous and stable point of view from which feminist political discourse moves. Instead, the aim is to recognize, in women's speaking out, the interruption of "man's social symbolic labor" that establishes "masculine and feminine and the relationships between them" and that makes the patriarchal valorization of women's bodies the "infrastructure" of a social order that Luce Irigaray has defined as "homo-sexual" by virtue of the claim of homologation and the unilateral character of that process of valorization (Irigaray, 1987 [1974]: 135; Irigaray 985 [1977]: 176). Sexual difference, therefore, does not designate an identity founded ontologically in the anatomy. Rather, as Alenka Zupančič argues, the political assertion by women against masculine domination and its material effects fractures the homogeneity of the social by making the division that constitutes it evident (Zupančič, 2017: 35).

In this sense, the concept of woman does not define a political identity which, as such, always and constantly bears the guilt of excluding others who do not recognize themselves as part of its definition. Moreover, its political and social relevance cannot be erased by affirming a plurality of gender differences that can proliferate through individual behaviors and practices, only insofar as they assume the ontological fixation of what a woman is within an oppressive binary matrix. The absence of the category of gender from the pages of this book is not the result of an irresponsible forgetfulness, nor does it intend to deny the importance of the political critique of society articulated by the so-called gender minorities and their social movements since the second half of the 20th century. Rather, it stems from the belief that gender politics – as well as queer politics – cannot find their legitimacy only in the binary opposition to heterosexuality, or even in the erasure of the name "woman", but must also be put to the test of the social conditions of its production. The reason for the absence of the category of gender is therefore the epistemological and political centrality recognized in the moments of insubordination in which millions of women have spoken out as women to reject the material position imposed on them by masculine domination. The concept of woman cannot be reduced to the signifier of oppression without erasing the struggle fought by women to re-determine its content starting from a claim to liberation. The concept of woman does not designate an identity, but an antagonism that breaks the identity imposed on women by masculine domination.

For this reason, the concept of woman is not a universal one, although in some historical passages it has undergone processes of universalization articulated through different discursive practices, which in all cases must be criticized. First of all, there is the claim to be integrated into existing society – as individuals entitled with rights, as working citizens or, more recently, as human capital capable of competing on the market according to the neoliberal logic of "lean in" – which had the effect of transforming a socially and historically determined figure of the sexed experience (the middle-class woman, the white bourgeois woman living in suburbs or the female self-entrepreneur) into the general and privileged referent of the political discourse supported by some

women and feminists.[4] Secondly, there are the practices of a radical feminism
that does not limit itself to considering the sexual oppression of women as
the matrix of any relationship of domination and subordination, but explicitly generalizes it as the common condition of all women beyond any social
determination of their positions. The third practice – expressed in an exemplary way by the Italian "feminism of difference" – consists in the symbolic
valorization of feminine difference which, while claiming to make a cut in the
patriarchal symbolic order, justifies the peremptory declaration that women
are alien to power.[5] Recognizing and describing these different strategies of
universalization does not mean putting them all on the same level, because
there is clearly an unbridgeable distance between a feminism that claims to
put an end to the subordination of women, one that explicitly invokes a complete subversion of existing power relations and a discourse that, embracing
the imperatives of the neoliberal program, claims for women "equal opportunities of domination" (Arruzza, Bhattacharya and Fraser, 2019). However,
each of these perspectives, in different ways and at different times, has opened
up a polemical front within feminism, made clear by the speaking out of those
women – black, workers, subaltern – whose sexed experience is marked by
racism, exploitation, poverty, and exclusion from the enjoyment of any rights.

The category of intersectionality has become central in contemporary feminist debate precisely because of the attempt to treat sexual oppression as one
of the many possible forms of oppression that concretely determine women's
lives.[6] The limit of this proposal, however, is that it criticizes the universalization of the concept of woman through a phenomenology of oppression
that indefinitely multiplies its manifold determinations and ultimately makes
them equivalent, and thus ends up neutralizing the antagonism triggered by
the politicization of that concept. Moving in another direction, albeit starting
from the same problem, this book treats the concept of woman as a socially
produced concept, whose politicization enables highlighting not only the individual axes of oppression that constitute it, but also and above all their systematic connection within the overall order of society.

This perspective explains why, in the following pages, the history of the concept of woman is not reconstructed either according to the chronological scan-
ning of "waves"[7] or with the pretension of giving back an exhaustive history of

---

4 Exemplary cases are Mary Wollstonecraft, which is discussed in the second chapter of this
book, Friedan, 1970 [1963] and Sandberg, 2013.
5 Cf. Muraro, 1996 [1992]; Diotima, 2009. On radical feminism see chapter 3. For a more recent
queer reconfiguration of the discursive practice of radical feminism, see Zappino, 2019.
6 See chapter 3.
7 Cf. Baritono, 2018; Hewitt, 2012.

feminism or feminisms. Rather, the concept of woman is treated as the fundamental indicator of the constitution of societal relationships and their contestation. In the transition from feudal society to modern commercial society
inhabited by free and equal individuals, in the heart of the slave and racist
society on which modern society is built, in the moment of the affirmation of
industrial capitalism and in the culmination of the Keynesian compromise,
during the neoliberal restructuring of society and the state and in the post-
colonial process of globalization of capital, the politicization of the concept
of woman makes it possible to consider masculine domination as a societal
operator which, while constituting a historical constant, an intrinsic necessity of every order, is historically configured in different ways. In the historical
movement of the concept of woman, therefore, the color line and the class
relationships that polemically divide the feminist front do not count as contingent attributes of sexual difference, but as its constitutive factors. Rather
than thinking of feminism according to a progressive logic ranging from the
claim of equality to the affirmation of difference, to the centrality achieved by
multiple differences, the intention of this book is to trace the moments within
history when women's claim to overthrow masculine domination transforms
feminism into a political practice of radical criticism of the very constitution
of society.

For these reasons, feminism is not classified in these pages according to
doctrinal canons, making it derive from the streams of thought from which
it should draw justification and historiographical dignity, in the same way Eve
came into the world from Adam's rib. By politicizing the concept of woman,
feminism has tormented those canons from within, showing their limits and
contradictions. Women's claim to be considered individuals with rights has
undermined the foundations of liberal discourse, revealing the sexed character of its subject and the sexual relationship of domination that makes his
freedom possible. Feminism has imposed a politicization of the private, and
a public and political presence of women that has overturned the republican
declination of the ideology of the "separate spheres". At every historical juncture, women have used the dominant political paradigms of their era – from
modern political theology to the social sciences of the nineteenth and twentieth centuries – re-articulating them within antagonistic tactics aimed at delegitimizing the patriarchal foundation of existing political and social relations.
In the twentieth century, Marxism was also polemically inhabited by feminism, which denounced the oblivion that it brought to women's reproductive
labor in the process of capital valorization, when it did not reduce the conflict
between men and women to a secondary contradiction placed in the waiting
room of communism. However, the politicization of the concept of woman

that moves these criticisms allows us to think of feminism starting from the
Marxian problem of partisan politics, i.e., in the light of a conception of the
political in which antagonism is not a function of the production of the political and social unity that puts an end to it, but rather persists by preventing
order from closing in on its unity.[8] Investigating the history of the concept of
woman thus means tracing, within social relations, the difference that questions their existence because its political affirmation is not admitted by those
very relations and their homogeneous reproduction.

On the edge of the fracture that feminism opens in history, the concept of
woman thus becomes the name of a 'global part'. It does not simply designate
the objective, differentiated, and changing condition of women within different social configurations, but establishes the partial perspective from which
to practice criticism. In the historical process of the constitution of the global
present, the politicization of the concept of woman makes it possible to show
how feminism accelerated and declared the death of the modern political universal, that is, the crisis of citizenship and of the process of democratic integration experienced by western societies after World War II ; it denounces the
simultaneously racist and patriarchal character of the neoliberal reorganization
of society and its institutions; it makes manifest the operativity of masculine
domination and its transnational articulation in the process of globalization
of capital and the state. On these different historical thresholds, feminism is
internally divided by polemical lines that cannot be either ignored or reconstructed as different stages of the same evolutionary movement, but instead
point to the persistence of questions that have not yet been answered. In its
collective, political, and social connotation, the concept of woman shows the
internal limits of the politics of rights and raises the question of how an emancipation is possible that does not constantly reproduce the patriarchal, racist
and proprietary articulation of social power, all the more so in the face of the
emergence of a "global state" that makes increasingly evident that the rights
claimed are irrecoverable. The politicization of sexual difference practiced by
feminism makes it necessary to think about the transnational reorganization
of the social and sexual division of labor in the face of movements of men
and women across borders that have no precedent in history. It also points
to violence against women as the most striking material manifestation of the
"man's social symbolic labor" that operates globally as a stable factor of imposition and legitimation of any social power relationship, of racism as well as
of exploitation. These questions make the feminist problem global not only

---

8   Cf. Ricciardi, 2019: 75.

because its political articulation by women has reached a planetary extension, but because it unavoidably affects the whole of society.

By attempting to answer these questions, feminism intensifies the universal promise of liberation contained in the concept of woman from the moment it historically affirms itself as a collective singular. In different ways, this promise is present in the political discourse of all women who speak out in this book. However, recognizing it does not mean naively attributing to every historical manifestation of the feminist discourse a revolutionary project, but refusing to consider it a "woman question" in order to bring its overall political implications to the fore. These become all the more pressing the more the perspective imposed by black women, workers, and subalterns who live and work in postcolonial contexts and in metropolises all over the world increasingly breaks the apparent unity of the collective singular. The fracture that furrows the concept of woman internally prevents feminism from being thought of as a separate issue, whose partiality is reduced to a politics of sex, or sexuality, which systematically erases the way in which racism and class relationships re-define the sexed experience. Precisely because it is a collective singular, the concept of woman does not allow for the unified representation of the subject of feminism, but points to the need to think of feminism as a practice of connection and confrontation between heterogeneous conditions that are both materially linked within the global capitalist order, and politically separate from the hierarchies and power relations that organize it. The truth affirmed by Sojourner Truth in nineteenth century US slave society must today be re-articulated by showing that women's liberation is not possible if social subordination persists, just as the emancipation of subordinates is inconsistent if women remain oppressed. This truth must continue to torment feminism in the face of the global society of capital, while it should still animate the conviction, nourished by Sojourner Truth, that women have the strength, if they act collectively, to "turn the world upside down".

References

Allen, M.P. (1997–2002) *The Concept of Woman*, 3 vols. Cambridge: W.B. Eerdmans.

Arruzza, C., Bhattacharya, T. and Fraser N. (2019) *Feminism for the 99%. A Manifesto.* New York: Verso.

Baritono, R. (2018) "Dare conto dell'incandescenza". Uno sguardo transatlantico (e oltre) ai femminismi del lungo '68. *Scienza & Politica. Per una storia delle dottrine* 59: 17–40.

Bourdieu, P. (2001 [1998]) *Masculine Domination.* Stanford: Stanford University Press.

Brown, W. (1988) *Manhood and Politics*. Totowa (NJ): Rowman &Littlefield.

Butler, J. (2010 [1990]) *Gender Trouble. Feminism and the Subversion of Identity*. New York – London: Routledge.

Cappuccilli, E. and Ferrari, R. (2016) Il discorso femminista. Storia e critica del canone politico moderno. *Scienza &Politica. Per una storia delle dottrine* 54: 5–20.

Diotima (2009) *Potere e politica non sono la stessa cosa*. Napoli: Liguori.

Dominijanni, I. (1995) Il desiderio di politica. In: Cigarini L., *La politica del desiderio*. Parma: Nuova Pratiche Editrice, 7–46.

Foucault, M. (1977) Entretien inédit entre Michel Foucault et quatre militants de la LCR, membres de la rubrique culturelle du journal quotidien *Rouge*. Available (consulted 23 March 2023) at: https://questionmarx.typepad.fr/files/entretien-avec-mic hel-foucault-1.pdf.

Friedan, B. (1970 [1963]) *The Feminine Mystique*. New York: Dell Publishing.

Galli, C. (2001) *Genealogia della politica. Carl Schmitt e la crisi del pensiero politico moderno*. Bologna: Il Mulino.

Hewitt, N.A. (2012) Feminist Frequencies: Regenerating the Wave Metaphor. *Feminist Studies* 3: 658–680.

Irigaray, L. (1985 [1977]) *This Sex which is not One*. Ithaca (NY): Cornell University Press.

Irigaray, L. (1987 [1974]) *Speculum. Of the Other Woman*. Ithaca (NY): Cornell University Press.

Koselleck, R. (1987) Historik und Hermeneutik. In: Koselleck R. and Gadamer H.-G. (1987) *Hermeneutik und Historik*. Heidelberg: Winter.

Koselleck, R. (2004 [1979]) *Futures Past. On the Semantics of Historical Time*. New York: Columbia University Press.

Loraux, N. (2006 [1997]) *The Divided City. On Memory and Forgetting in Ancient Athens*. New York: Zone Books.

Mitchell, J. (1966) *Woman's Estate*. Harmondsworth – Baltimore: Penguin.

Moi, T. (2008 [1999]) *What is a Woman?* Oxford: Oxford University Press.

Morrison, T. (1987) *Beloved*. New York: Alfred A. Knopf Inc.

Muraro, L. (2006 [1992]) *L'ordine simbolico della madre*. Roma: Editori Riuniti.

Okin, S.M. (1979) *Women in Western Political Thought*. Princeton: Princeton University Press.

Pateman, C. (2003 [1980]) *The Disorder of Women. Democracy, Feminism and Political Theory*. Cambridge: Polity Press.

Ricciardi, M. (2019) *Il potere temporaneo. Karl Marx e la politica come critica della società*. Milano: Meltemi.

Riley, D. (1995 [1988]) *"Am I That Name"? Feminism and the Category of "Women" in History*. Minneapolis (MN): University of Minnesota Press.

Rubin, G. (1997 [1975]) The Traffic in Women. Notes on the "Political Economy" of Sex. In: Nicholson L. (ed) *The Second Wave. A Reader in Feminist Theory.* New York – London: Routledge, 26–62.

Sandberg, S. (2013) *Lean In: Women, Work, and the Will to Lead.* New York: Alfred A. Knopf.

Schmitt, C. (2007 [1932]) *The Concept of the Political. Expanded Edition.* Chicago – London: Chicago University Press.

Scott, J.W. (1986) Gender: A Useful Category of Historical Analysis. *The American Historical Review* 91(5): 1053–1075.

Zappino, F. (2019) *Comunismo queer. Note per una sovversione dell'eterosessualità.* Milano: Meltemi.

Zupančič, A. (2017) *What is sex?* Cambridge (MS) – London: The MIT Press.

Acknowledgements

This book is the result of many years of work. I tried to reconcile analytical depth with expositive clarity as I learned from Carlo Galli, who communicated to me the importance of the genealogy of the political and discussed with me the concept of woman with all his scientific thoroughness. My first sincere thanks go to him. Eleonora Cappuccilli, Isabella Consolati, Roberta Ferrari, and Lucia Giordano have accompanied and made this book possible in many ways. I hope they know that they are present on every page. Matteo Battistini, Jacopo Bonasera, Matilde Ciolli, Luca Cobbe, Camilla De Ambroggi, Lorenzo Delfino, Francesca Della Santa, Felice Mometti, and Alessandra Spano have contributed to this work by discussing even the smallest details. Many other men and women have been part of the connections that have made this book possible: I am grateful to all of them. Raffaella Baritono pushed me to fill in the gaps, Maurizio Ricciardi indicated present possibilities and invited me to determine them. Without them, what I write would lack the privilege of collective thought. Finally, I want to thank Jacopo Bonasera and Annalisa Cananzi for their precious support for finalizing the manuscript, and Dave Mesing for his invaluable and tireless help in revising the English.

This book was written during the experience of the strike and the global women's movement against masculine violence, which every day shows the intensity and persistence of the feminist problem. I am indebted to all those who stubbornly keep the fracture open. Adriana, my mother, has been there at every step, as always. I dedicate this book to the memory of her mother Pina, a woman who ate every crumb of freedom and who, even in the most unlikely circumstances, sang.

On the Threshold of a New Order

1   The Announcement of a Difference

On February 1, 1402, Christine de Pizan wrote to Isabeau of Bavaria and Guillaume de Tignonville to bring them up to date on the discussion of the second part of the *Roman de la Rose*, the controversial work begun by Guillaume de Lorris and completed by Jean de Meun (Pizan, 2007 [1402a]). Until then, the debate had been between her, Jean Gerson, and Jean de Montreuil, the celebrated theologian and chancellor of the University of Paris and the first French humanist. Addressing the Queen of France and the provost of Paris, Pizan contravenes the rule of 'literary discretion' and highlights the political stake of the debate.[1] If the merit of a work can be justified only according to the utility of the "common good" [*la chose publique*], Jean de Meun's work is completely useless (Pizan, 2007 [1401]: 131). What is more, it is harmful: without any modesty, it encourages lust, while it launches "excessive, impetuous, and false accusations, insults, and defamation of women – whom he accuses of several great vices and perverse habits" (Pizan, 2007 [1401]: 125). In the face of this intolerable misogyny – a livorous reaction to the relative social mobility and freedom won by women in the late Middle Ages[2] – Pizan is outraged, ready to "defend the honor and praise of women" (Pizan, 2007 [1402a]: 109).[3] Hers is a real "war" that requires that the authoritative recipients of her appeal take a stand, all the more necessary because she has weak tools "against these illustrious and distinguished men" who celebrate Jean de Meun's novel (Pizan, 2007 [1402b]: 217). Pizan's tools are weak because she herself is a woman and must confront the beliefs and conventions of the era in which she lives. Even her speech is as unexpected as it is illicit: it violates the established and recognized authorial canon, it questions the male monopoly of knowledge and the hierarchies of an order of the world and society considered as fair as it is immutable. Pizan is a woman of her time and does not explicitly challenge that order. However, she opens a crack in it that is destined to widen as she asks herself "which women? Who are they?", finding within misogynistic literature

---

1   For an historical framing of the debate, see Hicks, 1977. On Pizan's work see at least the essay collected in Hicks, Gonzalez and Simon 2000; Zimmermann and De Rentiis 1994.

2   Cf. Opitz, 2017.

3   Cf. Kelly, 1982.

an answer that makes them "devouring beasts and enemies of humans" with the sole purpose of "deceiving and conquering them" (Pizan, 2007 [1402c]: 175). Therefore, when Pizan takes on the task of answering the question "who are women?", and when she offers a practical answer to that question based on her own experience as a woman, she openly accuses the masculine definition of her sex, showing that it is primarily an act of power.

In the eyes of her opponents, Pizan's speech is unacceptable. Gontier Col acknowledged her "high intelligence" but thought it "horrible" that a "woman passionate" could have the "manifest foolishness" and "pretentiousness" to amend Jean de Meun, "renowned philosopher, and expert in all seven liberal arts" (Col, 2007 [1401]: 135). According to Jean de Montreuil, "although she does not lack intellect, according to female capacity", Pizan is an arrogant woman (Montreuil, 2007 [1402]: 345). Pierre Col admits that he has heard of Pizan's "high intelligence, clear mind, and melodious eloquence", but then considers her arguments to be such that they do not even merit the response of Jean de Meun's lesser pupils (Col, 2007 [1402]: 307). These reactions can be considered the effect of a historical condition in which education was almost completely precluded for lay women, and in all cases – with rare exceptions among the ranks of the nobility – limited to the study of the doctrine of the Church and moral precepts.[4] The problem, however, is more radical and concerns not only the custom of the time, but the way in which it is justified. Indeed, Pizan's opponents establish a substantial identity between her sex, her intellectual minority, her exposure to the passions, and the subordination that follows. The arrogance of which she is accused coincides with her claim to rise above the position that nature imposes on her and that society reflects. Arrogance is, first and foremost, challenging a hierarchy that is ontologically justified and socially effective.

Pizan's first problem, therefore, is to legitimize her speaking out, and she does so with arguments that manifest her understanding of the terms of the confrontation. With a lucid rhetorical strategy, she describes herself as too "weak" to confront "such skilled masters" (Pizan, 2007 [1402a]: 109, 111) and presents herself to Montreuil as an "ignorant woman of inadequate opinion" [sentement leger] asking him to be lenient toward her "female weakness" (Pizan, 2007 [1401]: 119). On the surface, her words express acceptance of the minority attributed to her sex, but in fact, they reflect the conviction of her opponents for the sole purpose of overthrowing it. This is the purpose of her autobiographical account, the story of a woman moved by an ardent desire

---

4 Cf. Shahar, 2003.

for knowledge, who has cultivated her "love of learning and of a life of solitude" thus succeeding in collecting "the lesser flowers of the garden of delight"
(Pizan, 2007 [1401]: 119), fragments of knowledge that she has woven together
in such a way as to arouse wonder at her work, though "not because of its gran-
deur but because of its novelty, to which they were not accustomed" (Pizan,
2007 [1402c]: 189).[5] Pizan knows that she is a novelty, an unforeseen event in
the nature of things as much because of her erudition as because she spread
her works by becoming one of the first professional woman writers in history. When she acknowledges that she is extraordinary, however, she does not
intend to make an exception of herself, confirming the rule that establishes the
natural inferiority of women. Rather, the autobiographical account demonstrates that her starting point is not being a woman, but rather her experience
as a woman. In this way, her sex is no longer a weakness or a limitation, but the
source of legitimacy for her speaking out:

> For, to be sure, my purpose is simply to uphold the absolute truth because
> I know from experience that the truth is contrary to those things which
> I am denying. And as much as I am a woman, I am much better able to
> speak of these things than one who has no experience in this matter, and
> who thus can go only by mere assumption and guessing.
>
> PIZAN, 2007 [1401]: 129

The battle to challenge the identification of women with vice is a battle for
truth, which is first and foremost about its status. Pizan does not deny the
value of speculative knowledge and in fact explicitly argues "that in order
to speak about things properly, it is not necessary to have any experience"
(Pizan 2007 [1402c]: 147). Knowledge, however, is profoundly marked by sin,
which has generated a "worldly obscurity" that prevents one from learning in
their purity the secrets of the universal and infallible order imparted by God
to Nature (Pizan, 2007 [1402c]: 141). It is precisely the human inability to tap
into this eternal truth that generates the clash of opinions such as those that
diverge on the *Roman de la Rose*. Since an opinion is not affirmed "by established law" [*loy commandee*] but rather purely personal, there is no arrogance
in the act of criticizing it (Pizan, 2007 [1401]: 123, 125).[6] In this clash, sexed
experience can be considered decisive because what matters is not the knowledge of the secrets of the divine order – i.e., an inaccessible truth – or even

5 On Pizan's biography and work, see Kennedy, 1984; Muzzarelli, 2007; Willard, 1984.
6 On the centrality of opinion in Pizan's discourse, see Kelly, 2007.

"speaking about things properly" – i.e., a purely theoretical knowledge –, but the use and practical effects of discourse. The question "who are women?" is in no way about the universal content of the term woman, but about the space of action that it delimits.

This practical perspective is evident in Pizan's critique of the section of the *Roman de la Rose* in which Jean de Meun – by way of Reason – justifies the casual use of names designating male genitals. According to Meun, such use is not a sin, since they were created by God with the "marvelous intention" of "sustaining human nature" by ensuring generation. Moreover, it was not God but Reason that gave a name to his works in order "to increase our understanding", which means that the same thing could have a different name without changing in substance: if holy relics were called "testicles", they would continue to arouse the same devotion (Lorris and Meun, 1995 [1237–1280]: 133, 135). Pizan does not appreciate Meun's satire, and her answer is dry: "it is not the word which causes the disgrace of the thing, but the thing which renders the word disgraceful" (Pizan, 2007 [1401]: 121). The attributes of the thing spoken about are not deducible from God's intentions, which are absolutely pure and inaccessible, but from those of men. The term designating the male genitals is dishonest because mankind has all been made unclean by sin. One can pronounce a profligate name – as the Holy Scriptures do – with the intention of turning humanity away from the practice of vices or – as Meun does – to encourage them. One can speak of the genitals and use their name to be understood for the purpose of curing a disease, but that does not take away from the fact that their name is in itself disgraceful, because the world is marked by sin that has corrupted God's perfect work.

It is precisely the mark of sin that gives rise to qualities such as shame: this "was caused by the corruption of our first parents" who, in fact, as soon as they sinned and became aware of good and evil, covered their "secret parts" (Pizan, 2007 [1402c]: 145). In practice, therefore, what counts are the intentions, inclinations, and cognition of those who act. Cognition makes it possible to distinguish evil from good and arouses feelings, such as shame, which in turn are capable of governing behavior. Inclinations, on the other hand, can be deduced from actions, so that it can be said that Jean de Meun was full of "carnality" (Pizan, 2007 [1401]: 131), since he did nothing but encourage carnal love. Honorable women, on the contrary, would blush at his tales, cultivating "the noble virtue of shame, which by definition restrains obscenities and disgrace in word and deed" (Pizan, 2007 [1401]: 121). Experience, which gives Pizan the authority she needs to speak, shows that there are virtuous women in the world. Consequently, she cannot be considered arrogant for questioning, as a woman, the work of "such a skilled author" as Jean de Meun. Instead, it is the latter who is arrogant "when he alone dared to defame and to insult, without exception, an entire sex" (Pizan, 2007 [1401]: 133).

Just as sin establishes a ground of equality between women and men – inaugurating humanity's universal propensity for evil – so there is a practical difference that needs to be asserted to show the ethical inconsistency of any ontological distinction between the sexes. It is only from this perspective that it is possible to understand one of Pizan's most famous statements. In the auto-biographical section of her *Livre de la Mutacion de Fortune*, written between 1401 and 1403, Pizan states that she "became male" (Pizan, 2017 [1403]: 30) after the death of her husband, Etienne de Castel, left her as a widow who was responsible for three children and her mother. First, we meet the harmonious narration of her happy marriage, when at the court of Hymen her husband, a "new master", puts a ring on her finger and then guides her with the skill of an expert helmsman through the "great oceans", a metaphor for worldly life with its risks and dangers (Pizan, 2017 [1403]: 42).[7] Then there comes the tale of the grief that strikes her like a "storm", which has the tone of an epic adventure. Christine loses her senses and is ready to throw herself into the sea from the deck of the ship; then she resigns herself to the idea of dying, the pain so intense that it erases her fear as much as any other suffering, until Fortune – who out of envy of her happiness had inflicted such a hard, unmotivated loss on her – moved by compassion intervenes on her behalf:

> my mistress came to me ... and touched me all over my body. I remember well how she manipulated every limb and held them in her hands. ... I was entirely transformed. ... my flesh was transformed and stronger, my voice much fuller, and my body harder and quicker. I found my heart strong and bold, which astonished me, but I felt that I had become a true man ... I was very capable of making use of whatever was necessary to guide the ship ... I became a good master of the ship. I had to be that way, by necessity, in order to rescue myself and my household, if I did not want to die there. Thus I was a true man – it is not a fiction – capable of guiding ships. Fortune taught me that skill, and thereby took me from that situation.
>
> PIZAN, 2017 [1403]: 47

The metaphor of the helmsman – inspired by Plato and Aristotle – refers to a precise conception of the social and therefore political order, a hierarchical

---

7   On the use of the metaphor of stormy waters to represent Fortune, see Pitkin, 1999: ch. 4.

and ontologically established order that is to be governed optimally, but that in all cases cannot be changed. To this metaphor corresponds the one of the political body, which Pizan traces back to Plutarch but which she elaborates from a wider literature ranging from the apologue of Menenius Agrippa, of which Titus Livius gives an account, to the *Policraticus* of John of Salisbury: the three orders – nobles, knights, and people – are hierarchically arranged according to precise organic functions. At their head is the prince; knights and nobles "occupy the place of hands and arms"; the people are "the stomach, feet and legs" (Pizan, 1998 [1406–1407]: ch. 1).[8] The family also responds to this hierarchy, and in fact Etienne de Castel, as her husband, is the ruler of the small kingdom whose rudder he skillfully held as long as he lived. Within this order, as hierarchical as it is static, Pizan introduces an element of mobility that is made possible by the gap that exists between the intention and perfection of the divine work, its administration by Nature and its secular history. God makes the soul, a "celestial, a light, invisible spirit" which is "very knowing and attentive" because it contains all faculties: "understanding, memory, reasonable judgment". However, it is Nature that "arranges the body and readies it to receive the soul", and this may explain why those powers occur in different degrees, in different people: where the qualities of the soul are more developed, it must be assumed that the body is "better arranged". In short, Nature "allows or disallows the soul's good faculties to function [in the body], according to how the different tunings of the bodily instrument lead them" (Pizan, 2017 [1403]: 38). If the body establishes a limit to the exercise of the faculties disposed by God and thus determines the position each person occupies in the order of creation, in order to be able to act as a true man, to rule her family and learn the knowledge necessary to do so, in short to do something that a woman would not by nature have the capacity to do, Pizan must become a "natural man" [*homme naturel parfaict*] (Pizan, 2017 [1403]: 48).

In several passages, Pizan insists on the truth of her own marvelous adventure, asserting that "it is neither lie nor fable" or even a "dream", and invokes the myths of Ulysses and Circe, Tiresias and Iphis, to gather exempla capable of substantiating her tale. This insistence, however, reveals once again the rhetorical strategy of assuming and overturning the beliefs of her time, and therefore the ontological link between the nature of women and their possible and limited field of action. The story of her great mutation is in fact openly a metaphor that not only "does not exclude truth" (Pizan, 2017 [1403]: 43), but also and

---

8   On Pizan's conception of the political body, see Langdon Forhan, 2002: ch. 3. On the political metaphor of the helmsman, cf. Duso, 1999: 59–60; on the *analogia corporis*, see Piccinini, 2007: ch. 1.

above all allows for the prioritization of the practical and experiential status of truth. As Boethius – one of the references of the *Livre de la Mutacion de Fortune* – states, "wicked men are mental beasts in human bodies" (Boethius, 2008 [c. 524]: 120).[9] According to Boethius, the passage from one species to another is an indicator of a vicious action, in the same way that for Pizan, the transition from one sex to another is the sign of a transformation that pertains primarily to action. Although Nature distributes the faculties of the soul, which are in themselves perfect, through bodies, virtue and vice are practical attributes that depend on the use that each person makes of the faculties at his or her disposal: "we all have jewels [virtues], and if we do not use them, that is entirely our doing" (Pizan, 2017 [1403]: 39). Further, taking up Boethius again, Pizan believes that the body finds itself thrown into a worldly space and time that God – who is not interested in the distribution of earthly goods – has entrusted to the game of Fortune, a deity with two faces, envious and capricious, who has "infinite power over all finite things", over individuals as well as kingdoms, a power such that brings "many things to their opposite conclusion, even unexpectedly changing the forms of bodies" (Pizan, 2017 [1403]: 30). The world is not governed by divine justice but by chance, which can blindly strike even the virtuous or elevate to the highest heights of worldly honor and wealth those who have no merit. The infinite power of Fortune explains the great mutation of Pizan and makes it a real "miracle", an event that can go beyond nature because it projects nature into history (Pizan, 2017 [1403]: 104). This means that sexual difference is not relevant by virtue of its ontological specificity, but in relation to the fortuitous conditions that constitute it as a limit to the ability to cultivate the faculties of the soul:

> My mother [Nature] did so much for my father, however, that I resembled him in every way, right and truly, except only for my gender [*sexe*] ... But since I was born a girl [*fille*], it was not the norm that I would benefit in any way from my father's wealth [his knowledge] ... If justice ruled, the female would lose nothing in this regard, ... but I am absolutely certain that in many places, customs reign over justice. Therefore, due to a lack of learning, I lost out utterly on this very reach treasure. ... I desired it more than anything on earth, but that did not matter at all; things could only go according to the custom, may it be cursed by God!
>
> PIZAN, 2017 [1403]: 34–35

---

9 On the influence of Boethius in Pizan's reflection, see Falleiros, 2010.

Pizan's experience as a woman is first and foremost that of a passionate desire to cultivate her intellectual virtues put in check by worldly customs, which force her to settle for the crumbs of knowledge to appease her appetite. If, as Boethius argues, it is will and power that produce "any human action" (Boethius, 2008 [c. 524]: 109), Christine certainly did not lack the former. Nor did she lack power, that is, the ability necessary to dedicate herself to study, as evidenced by the results she was able to achieve. From her mother Nature, in fact, Pizan received not only beauty – an attribute that involves no discipline and therefore no merit – but also the faculty of discretion, the consideration necessary to deliberate, the virtue to "retain" what one has experienced and finally memory, the ability to recall that experience to mind (Pizan, 2017 [1403]: 37). Existing customs, therefore, cannot be justified from the alledged natural inferiority of women.

Further, the power to which Pizan refers is not simply a matter of one's own faculties, but of oppressive circumstances and conventions that transform woman's "fates" into a veritable martyrdom. It's not just about bad luck, which often "saddles her with a bad husband who wants to beat her" for specious reasons. On the contrary, it is the opinion of her weakness, which exposes her to the dishonor aroused by unjustified gossip, or to the flattery of those who try to induce her to shameful actions, or even to the greed of relatives and creditors lying ready to step forward to deprive a widow – who often cannot count on secular justice "if she does not have the means to pay up" – of the goods that she is entitled to inherit (Pizan, 2017 [1403]: 107–108). The misogyny of the clerics against whom Pizan wages her battle is as much the indicator as the factor of an earthly injustice that her experience as a woman allows her to reveal and denounce. In this way, her biography, the self-portrait of an extraordinary but not exceptional woman, inaugurates the narrative of the universal history she tells in the impressive *Livre de la Mutacion de Fortune*, a history driven, just like her life, by contingency and its vagaries.

From this perspective, it is possible to challenge, if not earthly hierarchies, at least the actions of those who, within those hierarchies, exercise authority and power. Visiting Fortune's castle, Pizan encounters political advisors whose malice, propensity to lie, and thirst for wealth and worldly honors she denounces (Pizan, 2017 [1403]: 93–95); after this, she meets the tutors of the sons of princes, flatterers who put their pupils on the wrong path and are unable to give them a good example (Pizan, 2017 [1403]: 95–96); the judges of the ecclesiastical courts, who abuse their power and are hostile to the poor; finally, the judges of the secular courts, who penalize those who do not have the means to demand justice and favor the nobles in their judgments (Pizan, 2017 [1403]: 96–97). As for clerics, they do not aspire to wisdom but to wealth, they are ignorant and prone to fallacious reasoning, elevated to their positions not by their valor – evidenced by study, prudence, wisdom, and love of knowledge – but only by the blind Fortune that despotically rules the world. Just as princes and nobles are born by pure chance into a position of power, so high prelates can ascend to the heights of the ecclesiastical hierarchy without any intervention of the Holy Spirit, but by a pure whim of fate (Pizan 2017, [1403]: 98–99).

Consistent with the medieval conception of Fortune articulated by St. Thomas and Boethius, Pizan does not abandon the idea of a providential design presiding over secular history. However, the world in which she lives, marked by the Western Schism and the crisis of both ecclesiastical and political authority that followed,[10] is not governed directly by God but by Fortune, who will be its "master" until her castle is burned down by the second coming of Christ (Pizan, 2017 [1403]: 92–99, 73–74). Further, like Boethius, Pizan also believes that virtue may not be rewarded on earth, yet the otherworldly character of salvation does not make virtue irrelevant in this world, nor does it entail resignation in the face of the omnipotence of providential design. Virtue may not be sufficient to take Fortune by the pigtails and beat her, tame her, and direct her – as it is a century later for Machiavelli (Machiavelli, 2008 [1513–1514]: 369); however, according to Pizan, virtue is certainly the condition for "resisting" Fortune [obviera male fortune] (Pizan, 2017 [1403]: 105). Therefore, in the hierarchical order of the earthly city, virtuous action opens an unexpected space even for a woman whom Nature had dressed up to prepare her for marriage and subject her to a "master" husband (Pizan, 2017 [1403]: 41). With her great mutation, Christine becomes a "master" in turn and, at the very moment she "becomes a true man", she loses the wedding ring that had sealed her domestic subordination (Pizan, 2017 [1403]: 47). The change in her body is a metaphor for a change that does not concern her being a woman, but her action and therefore the position she occupies in the world and its hierarchies.

Precisely because she insists on virtue as a practice, Pizan does not propose an image of female nature opposite and mirroring that artfully constructed by misogynistic clerics, and indeed rather bluntly acknowledges that there are also vicious and mischievous women. However, since "in general they are little involved in the essential dealings of government", their misdeeds contribute little to "worsen the state of the world" (Pizan, 2017 [1403]: 103). The reasons for this exclusion are not investigated in the *Livre de la Mutacion de Fortune*, where Pizan merely acknowledges the role of certain women – such as the

---

10   Cf. Van Engen 2008.

Amazons and Medea, Queen Semiramis and Helen of Troy – in the great fresco of universal history that she gives an account of in the work. However, this perspective changes considerably in *The Book of the City of Ladies*, where history is explicitly considered as a battlefield, the scenario of a one-sided war fought by men to consolidate and maintain their authority. For Pizan, rewriting history from the point of view of women is therefore a specific way of contesting the sexed relations of power that organize the knowledge, customs, and society of her time.

Again, the opening of the work reveals great rhetorical skill. Reading Matheolus' *Lamentations*, Pizan falls into prostration, curses having been born in a woman's body, regrets that God did not make her male so that "she would be as perfect as a male says he is". When he rushes to console her, Reason reproaches her for having believed "[men's] false testimony more readily than the certainty of [her] own identity". Experience is again invoked to establish the truth, but it is no longer just Christine's singular experience. On the contrary, it is her own and that of the "other women whose company [she] frequently kept", who had told her "their private experiences and intimate thoughts", women of all ranks whose stories together give her the authority to challenge "what men say", that is, a discourse whose credibility has rested on the silence of those it has placed in awe (Pizan, 1982 [1405]: 4–6). This time, what empowers Pizan in her speech is and must be the invocation of a common experience of women, so that the extraordinary character of her biography cannot be considered exceptional, and so that her perspective can become a different viewpoint on history.

The consequences are clear: first, the male monopoly of knowledge must be considered as much the effect of a power relationship as the condition of its continuity: "whoever goes to court without an opponent pleads very much at his ease. I assure you that women have never done what these books say!" There is a factual imbalance – "men are masters over their wives, and not the wives mistresses over their husbands" (Pizan, 1982 [1405]: 118–119) – which learned men justify by invoking natural and therefore unchangeable causes. Thus, for example, while men excuse their mistakes by asserting that "it is human nature to sin", when a woman errs then "it is completely a matter of fragility and inconstancy"; offences and insults are thus the foundation of the authority that men "confer upon themselves" [*ilz se donnent tele auctorité*] (Pizan, 1982 [1405]: 165). Recovering the doctrine of St. Augustine – in light of which there can be no such thing as a vicious nature, since nature is the work of God and reflects his perfection (Augustine, 2008 [413]: 249 and 2003 [422–426]: 142–143) – and reversing his conclusions regarding the subordination of women,[11] Pizan challenges the identification of her sex with vice by asserting that the soul was created "equally good and noble in the feminine and in the masculine bodies" (Pizan, 1982 [1405]: 23). It is true that the creator "ordained man and woman to serve Him in different offices, ... and to each sex has given a fitting and appropriate nature and inclination to fulfill their offices" (Pizan, 1982 [1405]: 31), but the fact that he created the woman's body from Adam's rib means that she "should stand at his side as a companion and never lie at his feet like a slave" (Pizan, 1982 [1405]: 23). The very signification of the female body made by men is therefore unveiled as a gesture of power: because women are weaker and more delicate, men have asserted that "the more imperfect a body, the lesser is its virtue" (Pizan, 1982 [1405]: 36). Rewriting history by starting from a gallery of women fighters opened by the terrible and noble Amazons serves to refute any specious naturalization of women's subjugation, starting with an experience that practically demonstrates their ability to exercise strength and boldness, in war as in government.

The difference of the body is not denied. What is rather denied are its practical and political effects. As Reason explains, nature compensates for the body's defects with other faculties, such as judgment and thought. One hundred and fifty years before Thomas Hobbes shapes modern political discourse, making politics an entirely human construction (Hobbes, 1985 [1651]: 183), Pizan must therefore affirm the artificial nature of domination in order to challenge its natural justification. Because what someone lacks in strength can be made up for by greater cunning, men and women must be considered naturally equal.[12] The exclusion of women from the administration of justice, therefore, does not depend on a defect in their intellect and inability to learn the law. The stories of virtuous queens and rulers, as well as of women who, having become widows, had to administer their own interests, show that "a woman with a mind is fit for all tasks". It is customs and habits which, by confining women to domestic occupations, have prevented them from diversifying their experience and thus developing their intellectual faculties. Whatever God's intention may have been, it is the public [*la chose publique*] that "does not require them to get involved in the affairs which men are commissioned to execute" (Pizan, 1982 [1405]: 32, 94).

The practical truth proclaimed by Pizan thus makes it possible to establish a political difference between the "common or public good" [*bien commun ou publique*], the "private or personal good" [*bien privé ou propre*], which

---

11   On Augustine and Pizan, see Walters 2000.
12   On Hobbes and Pizan, see Green 1994.

benefits only one part of the city or the political community, and finally the good obtained by one party to the detriment of the other, "a real extortion carried out arbitrarily" [*droicte extorcion*] (Pizan, 1982 [1405]: 187) that misogynist clerics legitimize and encourage. This consideration does not go so far as to claim the political participation of women, which in many ways is already a fact: there have been many women who have exercised government wisely, fairly, and bravely; just as many have contributed and continue to contribute to the establishment of the general good through their activities, whether they be extraordinary inventors who have opened up new fields of theoretical and practical knowledge, or ordinary women of low rank who, by working and supporting their husbands, ensure the harmonious progress of worldly affairs. Pizan makes visible what misogynistic discourse conceals, namely the presence of women as authors and actresses of history and turns history into a polemical field by revealing the action of power where the subordination of women is justified by men upon ontological basis.

Precisely because she thinks about nature historically, that is, within the conditions in which sexual difference acquires meaning as a possibility or as a limit, Pizan can give value to experience as a practice and a discipline of movement. From this perspective, it is no longer necessary to resort to the metaphor of the great mutation of the body: if the name of the noble and courageous Dido means "virago", if the activities in which the queen of Carthage excelled can be considered naturally masculine, this depends on the fact that this was historically the case (Pizan, 1982 [1405]: 95). What should be emphasized, first, is the possibility of women acting as women off the path laid out for them in a world dominated by men and their discourse. Second, to historicize nature means to point to a possibility of transformation. The past crystallized in tradition and custom has a weight that must be confronted, but it does not mortgage the present or preclude the possibility of amending its injustice finally made evident:

> In the long run, everything comes to a heat at the right time, for how could God have long tolerated in the world heresies against His holy law, which were eradicated with such great difficulty and which would still persist today if they had not been challenged and overcome? It is the same with many other things which were tolerated for a long time, but which were then debated and disproved.
>
> PIZAN, 1982 [1405]: 185

By speaking out, Pizan opens a crack in the order because, from her own experience as a woman, she establishes the legitimacy of her mutation against the discourses that justify her status. Her experience, therefore, not only authorizes her to speak, but also allows her to challenge the authority that has silenced women like her, to the point of exclaiming "let all writers be silent who speak badly of women, let all of them be silent ... let them lower their eyes, ashamed for having dared to speak so badly, in view of the truth which runs counter to their poems" (Pizan, 1982 [1405]: 80). It should not be excluded that Alberico Gentili knew Pizan's 'internationalist' work – which had had considerable circulation in England – and was inspired by it when he ordered silence from theologians guilty of speaking *in munere alieno*, that is, without knowledge of the truth with which they were confronted, which was practical and changeable, not substantial and eternal (Gentili, 1993 [1612]: 92).[13]

Pizan, however, must tactically make use of the same discourse on which her opponents draw in order to authorize her own speech, a discourse that fully expresses the order of her time and that for this reason also continues to present itself as a limitation. Particularly at the moment when she makes use of a theological-political argument, she takes advantage of the space opened by the assumption of the equality of souls, but at the same time she comes up against an imperative of order that resists any experiential refutation. As a result, the ontological foundation of the sexual division of labor – which excludes women from politics in order to assign them to the loom – seems to resist any historicization, and indeed, as Rectitude tells Christine, investigating its causes would be endless work. Without further explanation, the belief in an inscrutable order that assigns each sex its place in God's service returns in the final exhortations of *The Book of the City of Ladies*, when Pizan declares – under the auspices of Justice – that "sometimes it is not the best thing for a creature to be independent" (Pizan, 1982 [1405]: 255), therefore recommending that wives not be disdainful of their domestic submission and practice the virtue of patience and forbearance.

In the Europe that preceded the Protestant Reformation but was already shaken by the effects of the Western Schism, the importance of works for the salvation of the afterlife intertwined with the emerging humanistic culture, laying the foundations for a non-substantialistic conception of virtue, which in turn made room for an action capable of questioning the natural, given, and immutable character of earthly roles and hierarchies, starting with the sexed ones. Her own doctrinal premises, however, lead Pizan to value the experience of subjection as martyrdom, which can be witnessed not only by

---

13   Concerning the circulation of Pizan's work in England, see Carrol, 1998; about Alberico Gentili, see Galli, 2009: 72–92.

the biographies of the saints she gives an account of in *The Book of the City of Ladies*, but also by every single wife who accepts being beaten in knowing that the prize for her patient acceptance is not of this world (Pizan, 1982 [1405]: 255). Sacred history – no less than profane history – thus bears witness to women's ability to practice virtue, and shows that Pizan's rewriting of history also moves within a canon, that of the *historia magistra vitae*, which derives its legitimacy from an appeal to tradition, assuming an ever-changing nature and thus the repeatability of events.[14] Compared to that tradition and its natural foundation – which inexorably confirms the subordination of women – even the virtuous inhabitants of the City of Ladies risk confirming themselves as exceptions to the eternally valid rule that decrees the inferiority of women.

Within this narrow framework, however, one cannot underestimate the novelty of the point of view introduced by Pizan, which is provided neither by Scripture, nor by the doctrine of the Church Fathers, nor by tradition. She makes use of an Augustinian conception of history by substituting for the perspective of God – who orders the events of the earthly civitas and gives them meaning in the history of salvation – that of women, who can thus finally afford to judge secular history by taking advantage of the empty space between divine justice and the contingency that governs the world.[15] While the divine order remains inscrutable, experience allows us to affirm that the regular succession of earthly events formalized by tradition does not decree destiny. The conditions for transforming the present, however, are still far off. In order to speak, Pizan invokes the extraordinary experience common to her and to many women of past and present times. That experience, however, is not yet a collective fact claimed as such by many women together with the aim of practically subverting an order built on oppression. Despite this, Pizan is able to show that the question "who are women?" does not find its ultimate answer in the masculine definition of the term, that there is a possibility to contest it and thus to reject the position it enshrines. This possibility should not concern only a few women capable of taking advantage of their freedom – the widows to whom, not surprisingly, the last lines of *The Book of the City of Ladies* are addressed – but all women. In order for them to finally grasp it, a great change is necessary and must involve both those who intend to practice it and all the relationships that determine the space of their action.

---

14   Cf. Koselleck, 2004 [1979]: 30.
15   Cf. Rudan, 2016.

2   Nature in Motion

More than two centuries after the debate around the *Roman de la Rose*, a copy
of *The Book of the City of Ladies* lands across the Channel, becoming part of
Margaret Cavendish's library.[16] Many things have changed since it was written: the providential order of the world has been shaken by the civil wars of religion; the modern political discourse to which Hobbes gives the first complete
formulation sees the light in the midst of a disorder in which women, preachers
and sectarians are unexpected protagonists. In this scenario of great transformation, the eccentric Duchess of Newcastle, trying her hand at the masculine
art of rhetoric, brings the *querelle des femmes* back into vogue and turns it into
one of the "most serious and most concernable" subjects for mankind on a par
with war and peace, commerce and government (Cavendish, 1662: *A Præfactory
Oration*).[17]

In her *Orations of Divers Sorts*, published in 1662, Cavendish traces a path
for her readers along which two men meet to discuss female freedom in the
public square. On the same path, there is also a group of women, who, after
having listened to the men, meet in private to discuss their own condition.
The question "what is a woman?" resounds in these pages without finding an
answer. Although they are on opposite sides – the first condemns female freedom, the second reclaims it – the men share the same perspective: the use-
fulness and harm of that freedom must always be thought of in relation to
the property and reputation, as well as feelings and desires of the men themselves. For their part, women oscillate between the lament for a condition of
misery and the satisfaction of being maintained, desired, and pleased by men;
between the conviction that nature has made women "witless and strengthless" (Cavendish, 1662: 227–228) and the certainty that this very inferiority
brings the advantage of not having to engage in the toils of work, the risks of
war, the wear and tear of university studies. Amid this oscillation, two speakers
argue that nature can be transformed and that it is impossible to know oneself
"before made a trial". If it is true that women are "witless and strengthless", it is
only because "strength is increased by exercise" (Cavendish, 1662: 228) and wit
by conversation, of which they have been deprived. If it is true that men are "a
degree in nature more perfect", "to imitate men" is not an act against nature,

---

16   Cf. Malcolmson, 2002.

17   On women's political presence during the first English Revolution, see Cappuccilli, 2015;
      about the *querelle des femmes* see Bock, 2002: 1–31.

but an opportunity to perfect oneself through the practice of one's faculties (Cavendish, 1662: 228–230).[18]

It is not easy to determine Cavendish's position in this diatribe, because contradictory arguments are present in her works, which assert the natural equality between men and women and consider masculine domination an "usurpation" and a "tyrannical government", but at the same time acknowledge a natural difference between the sexes in terms of intellect and physical strength, thus justifying both masculine domination and that "Man is made to Govern Common Wealths, and Women their private Families" (Cavendish, 1655: *Preface to the Reader*). With certainty, however, it can be said that Cavendish is not content to contrast the disparaging masculine definition of "what is a woman" with what women actually do, demonstrating that they are capable of practicing the virtues (Cavendish, 1655: 73); nor is she interested in formulating a definition that mirrors that offered by men. Her problem is to clarify that nature which is invoked to affirm both equality and difference between the sexes, what its rules of operation are, and whether those rules really establish a hierarchy between men and women. From this "search for truth" flows a conception of nature as a movement that prevents any ontological fixation of positions and any theological justification of domination. The question "what is a woman?" is answered in the social communication that determines the content of the concept, showing the patriarchal foundation of modern politics just as much as its inevitable instability.

If *ars rhetorica* is hostile to women, natural philosophy is no less so, and it is not surprising that Cavendish has to justify her own bold intrusion in this field of knowledge.[19] When in 1664 she tried her hand at writing the *Philosophical Letters*, she therefore put into practice a complex strategy of affirmation. This provides first of all the election of an interlocutor as imaginary as authoritative, a Lady to whom she asks to take a stand and "vindicate" her if she happens to hear someone throw "accusations and blemishes" on her work (Cavendish, 1664: 136). Secondly, the Duchess relies on the support of her husband William, who used to introduce his wife's works with a short sonnet as a seal of approval.[20] The most important element of Cavendish's authorial strategy, however, lies in her invocation of the "novelty" of her opinion compared to that of her counterparts – authors such as Thomas Hobbes, René Descartes,

---

18   On Cavendish's *Female Orations* cf. Rudan, 2015.
19   On Cavendish's natural philosophy see Sarasohn 2010; Siegfried and Sarasohn; 2014; Walters, 2014: ch. 1.
20   On the role played by "conjugality" in Cavendish's work, see Lilley, 2003.

the Dutch chemist Jean Baptiste van Helmont, and the Cambridge Platonist Henry More – which makes her writing compelling:

> to find out a Truth, at least a Probability in Natural Philosophy by a new and different way from other Writers, and to make this way more known, easie and intelligible, I was in a manner forced to write this Book.
>
> CAVENDISH, 1664: *To His Excellency the Lord Marquis of Newcastle*

Cavendish's speaking out is justified by virtue of the difference she wishes to assert. The ritual *excusatio* to readers – in which the author makes explicit her own ignorance, recalls that she is uneducated in the arts she discusses, asks for indulgence for flaws in knowledge due to her sex – actually defines a privileged viewpoint on the world and its phenomena because it is unexpected and unpredictable for the scientific canon of her time. Thus, the rationalism of Hobbes and Descartes – the identification of intellect and language as a specifically human feature from which follows the inevitable conclusion that "man is a Monopoler of all Reason" – is not only questionable because it ignores and therefore denies the different ways in which knowledge can arise in nature, but also and especially because it legitimizes an entire system of hierarchies. While acknowledging, like Hobbes, that all men (and women) are equally endowed with "sense and reason", it is indeed necessary to admit that in some reason can be better regulated, allowing them to "over-power the other" (Cavendish, 1664: *Preface to the Reader*).[21] Even when it moves from a petition of equality, therefore, natural philosophy in fact expresses a relationship of domination. Invoking the monopoly of language and therefore of reason, man elevates himself to the "measure" of all things, both of other creatures and of those of his own species (Cavendish, 1664: *Preface to the Reader*) and performs an unacceptable act of "presumption and arrogancy" that for Cavendish coincides with an exclusive "adscription of power" (Cavendish, 1664: 278, 309). The male prerogative of practicing natural philosophy then allows the name "man" to be considered not as a generic reference to the human species [*Man-Kind*], but as an indicator of a sexed being, and is the historical premise from which the novelty of the perspective embodied by Cavendish is evident. This novelty consists in the speech of one who – because of her sex – is not legitimized to speak about science, but who by the very act of speaking demonstrates that she can exercise her intellect in the search for the truth of nature. The masculine monopoly of language and rationality is questioned, its "partial" character

---

21   About Cavendish and Hobbes see Ankers, 2003 and Rudan, 2020.

is exposed, and man who thinks of himself as God is reduced to "a small finite part of Infinite Nature" (Cavendish, 1664: 147, 278).

Cavendish is aware that her speaking out may be a source of dispute. In her dedicatory letter to her husband, she expresses her doubt that he might disapprove of her choice to write, since hers is a "Book of Controversies" and any controversy risks turning friends into enemies (Cavendish, 1664: *To His Excellency the Lord Marquis of Newcastle*). Against the background of this fear, the clamor of the recently concluded civil war resounds, which the spouses from Newcastle – forced into a long exile because of their convinced loyalty to the Stuarts and because of the political role played by William at the court of Charles I – had paid dearly in terms of money and prestige.[22] It is therefore a question of defining the field of confrontation by distinguishing between natural philosophy and theology, hence avoiding talking about God except when philosophical arguments require it. By drawing the boundary of the discourse, Cavendish aims to neutralize and govern the polemical effects of the free interpretation of the Scriptures. Even if nothing can repress or constrain the freedom of thought, in matters of faith it is necessary to stick to the only true interpretation of the word of God, which, according to her, is the one offered by the established Church (Cavendish, 1664: 208–211), so much so that the *Blazing World* of her own creation – where the Emperatress converts the subjects to her own religion – was organized according to the principle *cuius regio, eius religio* (Cavendish, 2003 [1666]: 87). Christ's commandment – "give to God what is Gods, and to Cæsar what is Cæsars" (Cavendish, 1664: 221–222) – not only defines a principle of "simple obedience" to constituted authorities, as it does for Hobbes (Hobbes, 1985 [1651]: 259),[23] but also entails a specific scientific corollary that consists in distinguishing "what belongs to the actions of Nature, and what to the actions of Religion" (Cavendish, 1664: 221). Only nature – that is, the material essence of man – can be known. Since the essence of God is immaterial, he is incomprehensible and can only be the object of faith (Cavendish, 1664: 3, 211, 225).

Cavendish's, therefore, is a declaration of obedience to the doctrine of the established Church, a gesture of submission that, through her practice of natural philosophy, results in an act of insubordination: acknowledging that God is "the God of Order" (Cavendish, 1664: 226) and declaring absolute obedience to him coincide with the dismissal of man from the position of lord of nature, with the contestation of his earthly dominion and with an opening – which

---

22   Cf. Whitaker, 2004: 234 ff.
23   About Hobbes' conception of the Christian State, see Galli, 2011: XXV ff.

anticipates Mary Astell's theological-political move – to the possibility of criticizing the knowledge and power derived from the male monopoly of knowledge.

If truth is not the product of reason – which at most can give "confirmation" –, if there can be no perfect knowledge in nature because perfection concerns only God and if, eventually, obligation is not questioned because authority, not truth, is that which makes the law, then truth as "probability" can be the object of a continuous "inquisition" in which the expression of a variety of opinions is legitimate (Cavendish, 1664: 341). Rationality, for Cavendish, is limited: it finds the rules that govern the movement of nature and its manifestations but does not establish them through the exercise of an absolute sovereignty. This is why natural philosophy does not produce certainty, but only opinions. Starting from these assumptions, the Duchess of Newcastle can put herself at the same level of the natural philosophers with whom she confronts, because even in dissent she shares with them the rules that govern the clash (Cavendish, 1664: *To His Excellency the Lord Marquis of Newcastle*). This does not mean denying or neutralizing the power of opinions – which, during the civil wars of religion, had manifested themselves in all their destructive force – but rather investigating their reasons, starting from a fully immanent conception of nature and its movements.

Underlying Cavendish's philosophical opinion is the idea that there is "not onely a Sensitive, but also a Rational Life and Knowledge, and so a double Perception in all Creatures" (Cavendish, 1664: *To His Excellency the Lord Marquis of Newcastle*). The influence of Renaissance humanism – like that of Tommaso Campanella[24] – and the intellectual climate of the United Provinces – where the Duchess spent most of her exile gravitating around the "Newcastle Circle" – determined a conception of nature as a "substance" common to all creatures. Among them there are no substantial differences then, but only a different participation in the rational and sensitive matter, which is always corporeal and can therefore be divided and combined in different ways. Nature is a substance in constant motion, whose infinite empirical manifestations neither produce nor justify any hierarchy, but only an infinite variety. The common laws of nature condense into a single law, which is "to keep infinite matter in order" (Cavendish, 1664: 146). Since every single movement of matter is an expression of its inherent wisdom, nothing can be called "unnatural". Every phenomenon – peace, war, enjoyment and pleasure, affliction or pain, life and death – is embedded in a single movement of nature that is always

---

24   Cf. Nicolosi, 2008: 39.

"regular" and may at most manifest some "irregularities" in its individual parts (Cavendish, 1664: 234 ff), where the irregularity consists of "not usual" alterations from an otherwise usual course, of oppositions that may even express themselves as a conflict, but which are not such as to deny the inherently peaceful character of nature itself, the infinite wisdom that presides over its movement (Cavendish, 1664: 228).

The consequences of this conception of nature are important. In the first place, and as we have partly anticipated, it makes it impossible to attribute to man, in the twofold sense of the word, a superiority over all other creatures by assuming that he alone is endowed with rationality. It is also impossible to establish a pre-eminence of one part of the body – the head – over all the rest, starting from the erroneous presumption that rationality is concentrated in the brain and not, instead, diffused in all the limbs. Further, it is impossible to establish a separation between mind and body, as Descartes claims in his *Discourse on the Method* (Descartes, 2006 [1637]: 29), and Hobbes with him: this opinion derives from the "abstraction of Motion from Matter", as if motion was "an immaterial thing ... but not a bodily substance". On the contrary, for Cavendish "whatsoever is Immaterial, is Supernatural, Therefore Motions, Forms, Thoughts, Ideas, Conceptions, Sympathies, Antipathies, Accidents, Qualities, as also Natural Life, and Soul, are all Material" (Cavendish, 1664: 12). Although rational and sensible movements have their own characteristics, an "interior nature", it is not possible to separate them because they are "diffused and intermixt throughout all the body" (Cavendish, 1664: 52–56, 111–112).[25] While implicitly attacking one of the main arguments used to justify the inferiority of women – their inability to rationally dominate their sensitive and impulsive part, which in fact for her can be guided by reason, but at the same time inevitably influences it (Cavendish, 1655: *The Epistle*) – Cavendish affirms a fundamental principle of equality:

> It is impossible, that one single part should be King of the whole Creature, since Rational and Sensitive Matter is divided into so many parts, which have equal power and force of action in their turns and severall imployments; for though Nature is a Monarchess over all her Creatures, yet in every particular Creature is a Republick, and not a Monarchy; for no part of any Creature has a sole supreme Power over the rest.
>
> CAVENDISH, 1664: 337

---

25   On Cavendish's conception of motion, see Peterman, 2019.

The traditional use of the metaphor of the political body, also at work in Pizan's reflection, is reversed. Cavendish, in fact, does not affirm a conception of the body as a composition of functionally distinct organic parts arranged hierarchically to justify a particular organization of government, but on the contrary treats the form of government as a metaphor that allows one to explain the functioning of the body as a system of parts all equally subject to nature. This conception of the body then reverberates in a principle of cooperation whereby "no Creature can subsist alone and of it self, but all Creatures traffick and commerce from and to each other, and must of necessity do so, since they are all parts of the same Matter" (Cavendish, 1664: 421). The reversal accomplished by Cavendish marks a significant distance from Hobbes. Undoubtedly, the Duchess shares his egalitarian assumptions, namely that there are no stable natural relations of domination that can be justified from the existence of substantial differences between individuals. However, if all men had the same faculties, as he claims, then they would all be equally philosophers or fools. Once the existence of a substance common to all creatures is recognized, Cavendish's problem is to understand the movement of that substance, from which arise not only different creatures, but also differences between creatures of the same species, each acting "according to their proper natures" (Cavendish, 1664: 114) and within relationships of cooperation and social exchange from which it is impossible to make abstraction. In other words, for the Duchess, nature is not, as for Hobbes, a 'state', i.e., a condition resulting from a philosophical abstraction, but a movement that can only be understood through its changing empirical manifestations.

The question of women's freedom should be reread from this perspective, which philosophically synthesizes the disordered set of observations that Cavendish had developed in previous years by "making the World [her] Book" (Cavendish, 1655: *The Epistle*). In the *World's Olio*, a great fresco of the world represented in short sketches, aphorisms, and sonnets, the Duchess had in fact observed that in some nations women have greater freedom than in others: "not that those Nations are less sensible of the honour of Constancy in that Sex than the others, but that they are more confident of their Virtue and Chastity" (Cavendish, 1655: 74). Virtue is not considered as an intrinsic attribute of being – a quality naturally present or absent in the female sex – nor even simply as a practice, but is instead related to a shared "confidence" that may vary according to circumstances. The dynamics of how this confidence operates is evident in the treatment of adultery. According to Cavendish, the effects of a wife's infidelity involve everyone close to the adulteress. Because she is "dishonored", honest women will avoid her company. Her daughter will also be dishonored, since the consequences of the adulteress' conduct will spill over to her offspring as well. Finally, her husband will be dishonored, because he who has chosen a woman of no worth will be demoted in the "the Esteem ... of the World" (Cavendish, 1655: 75). This dishonor has material reasons: infidelity, in fact, "abolisheth all lawfull and right Inheritance", which should be based on the certainty of descent while instead, according to existing laws, "the Child that is born in Wedlock, although begot by another Man, shall inherit the Husbands Estate, although it be known to be another Mans". As a side effect, a man might be less industrious, fearing that the fruits of his labor will go to a son who is not his, while natural affection, parental tenderness, and strictness toward offspring would be weakened by suspicion, leaving room for disobedience by children (Cavendish, 1655: 76). The virtue and chastity of women are therefore evaluated and judged in relation to the function attributed to the family, marriage, and its hierarchies in the reproduction of order:

> Then for The Weal publick, which is as The great Wheel in a Clock, so every private Family is as The little Wheel for The Wealpublick; if a Man and his Wife disagree, which is want of Affection, Then Their Children, when They are grown up, begin to grow Factious, Some siding with The Mother against The Father, and others with The Father against The Mother; which Custome will make Them grow Factious in The Weal-publick, as well as in The Weal-private.
>
> CAVENDISH, 1655: 80

The dynamic of "confidence", the formulation of what can be called a socially shared judgment about women, is presented as the effect of this functional relationship between family and government. The double meaning, public and private, of the term "weal" – a good that shares the same root as wealth – shows that the "esteem of the World" for women is defined in light of the position they are called to occupy within specific dynamics of transmission of property and reproduction of authority. Answering the question "what is a woman?" is therefore a political problem precisely because the definition of the content of the concept is the result of these dynamics. Thinking of nature as motion and social exchange, Cavendish brings the Hobbesian conception of paternal power to its logical consequences: the latter is a private fact that for this very reason has public relevance, since the family is a fundamental cog in the overall functioning of the Commonwealth. The logical abstraction made by Hobbes – who, in order to affirm a radical principle of equality, imagines individuals coming into the world "like *Mushromes*", thus erasing the role of women in procreation and the sexual warfare that determines their subjection (Hobbes, 1987 [1642]: 117) – presupposes and hides the relationship of domination that underlies the unity of the sovereign order and that the Duchess makes manifest instead, making it a central element for the understanding of authority and its reproduction.[26]

Focusing on the functional relationship between the family and the Commonwealth, Cavendish argues that in both cases authority must be exercised by a single head. The recovery of the metaphor of the political body here does not serve to legitimize the prerogatives of government from the idea that they belong to those who hold the primacy of rationality, but responds to a criterion of effectiveness: a single "head" leading government guarantees the predominance of a single opinion, where precisely multiple "Opinions breed Disputations, and Disputations Factions, and Factions breed Wars, and Wars bring Ruin and Desolation" (Cavendish, 1655: 205). This observation is not so much important because it explains Cavendish's favor for monarchical government, but rather because of the centrality that opinions hold within her discourse, charging it with a polemical content. For her, the reproduction of obligation – be it political or familial – cannot rest simply on coercion, but must be based on a subjective adherence to the principle of authority and, consequently, on freedom: "The greatest Monarch that is Most beloved of The subject, because he hath not onely The power over mens bodies, but over Their minds ... The minde is a rebel, and stands out against him, thus freedom makes obedience" (Cavendish, 1655: 49). In this problematic framework, Cavendish's unseemly speaking out on natural philosophy acquires a precise political significance, since the social exchange that determines the meaning of the concept of woman becomes one of the necessary props to guarantee both the material conditions of existence of the government, and the subjective adherence of those subject to it.

Also in this regard, Cavendish confronts Hobbes' discourse, making her own the idea that the mind is always unsatisfied and that it is "alwayes running, but never comes to an end" (Cavendish, 1655: 40). In Hobbes, this anthropological premise justifies the necessity of the sovereign command, which in the very moment of its institution neutralizes – at least formally – the problem of opinions and their polemical character, relegating them to the internal forum and thus to an exclusively private freedom.[27] For Cavendish, on the contrary, opinions are politically central precisely because they arise from social exchange, from the "traffick" in which private individuals are necessarily immersed and which continues operating once the government has been established. For

---

26 Concerning the institution of paternal power in Hobbes' discourse see Schochet 1967, Pateman 1988: 44.

27 On the role of opinion in Hobbes' thought, cf. Bonasera 2019.

there to be authority and obedience, each person must be persuaded that he or she can be content with his or her position. Rebellion, in fact, is caused precisely by "the unequal living of the subject" (Cavendish, 1655: 51), a formula by which Cavendish does not mean the material inequality of their conditions, but the aspiration to have more than is convenient and appropriate to each person's rightful place. It is this excessive aspiration that spreads pride, ambition, envy, and factions, leading to civil war.

The subordination of women in the family therefore responds to the need to 'communicate' to children the necessity of subordination, continually legitimizing the existence of authority and thus preventing their minds from becoming factional. In order for this dynamic of social communication to operate, women themselves must be educated to prevent them from falling into the vortex of ambition; they must be shown "how beneficial and necessary Justice and Propriety is to the orderly Life of Man" (Cavendish, 155: 74). Justice and property consist in the recognition of the necessity of occupying the position appropriate to an order that is significantly presented as the opposite of civil war, that "corrupts good Manners, especially Women ... [and] makes Them believe Their own Praises, and yield to Flattery, The Murtherer of chastity" (Cavendish, 1655: 75). The social valorization of feminine virtues, therefore, is nothing but the reflection of an ordinary dynamic within which each person must be subjectively convinced of the justice of his or her own position, however subordinate, and accept it without exorbitant demands. It can thus be said that, for Cavendish, the subordination of women is not "natural" because it derives from a specific physical conformation or condition of their being, but rather because it is prescribed by an order in which it serves to guarantee both the regular transmission and accumulation of wealth, and adherence to a principle of authority and its continuity over time. Only within the semantic framework in which nature becomes the name of an ordinary social exchange can the Duchess claim that, when it "works perfectly", nature gives men properly "masculine" qualities – such as a valiant heart, a healthy body, the ability to be the head of a wife – and women properly "Effeminat" qualities – such as chastity, modesty, sobriety, and grace (Cavendish, 1655: 84).

Although the subordination of women is no longer justified on ontological grounds, but from the ordinary empirical manifestation of the movement of nature, it is still subordination. However, starting from these assumptions, Cavendish identifies spaces of freedom that show, if not the intrinsic instability, at least the openness to the transformation of private – and therefore political – relations that make up the gears of the Commonwealth. With a lexicon and attitude clearly inspired by Machiavelli, the Duchess recognizes the possibility for women to sovereignly govern their own behavior:

but a woman that would preserve her reputation, by fame as well as by chastity, she must put on as Many several faces, and behaviours as a State doth; for a State in time of war puts on a face of anger; and in time of plague and pestilence, a face of pietie, after rebellion a face of clemency; in times of peace and plenty, a face of mirth and jollity; so women must put on as Many behaviours, as she meets with several humours.

CAVENDISH, 1655: 32

The problem of reputation presupposes the dynamics of social exchange that preside over the formation of opinions, but at the same time sets it within changing conditions in which women have as much freedom to choose how to behave as they do to engage in behaviors that are unexpected with respect to socially recognized conventions. Thus, starting with the Machiavellian postulate that "it is Time and Occasion that makes Most things Good or Bad" (Cavendish, 1655: 81), Cavendish goes so far as to propose among the useful precepts for a married woman the idea of trying her hand at ordinarily masculine activities, such as hunting and riding, swimming, and wrestling, if it serves to please her husband. This small example of *specula mulierum* offers women margins of action that, while remaining formally limited by the due subordination to the marital authority, in fact circumvent the constraints defined by the social exchange that, as we have seen, when it operates "perfectly" puts everyone in their place, distributing to women and men characteristics appropriate to their position. A masculine woman, therefore, can be considered "defect" of nature, but is also at the same time a possibility intrinsic to her own motion: if it is true that "neither can any natural body get more strength than by nature it hath" (Cavendish, 1664: 442), then even one who, like Cavendish, acts outside the ordinary and invades a field conventionally belonging to men can be considered a natural woman, because she does something she has the power to do.

In this way, nature ceases to be a limitation for women, becoming the name of a set of viable possibilities that cannot simply be crushed or repressed without jeopardizing ordinary social exchange and the principle of authority it supports. Indeed, the postulate that matter and motion are not separable implies that the body "cannot quit power" (Cavendish, 1664: 98), and consequently that absolute power cannot arise in nature. Its extension is always defined within a relationship, whose terms – such as "a Master and his Servant, and a King and his Subjects" – are "relative" and must be thought of simultaneously (Cavendish, 1664: 16). Power is given where the movement of nature allows some to attain sufficient strength to "over-power" others. Obedience is given where the free will of each one is hindered or prevented by a superior power, which nevertheless does not cancel out that freedom (Cavendish, 1664: 97).

The "private family" is such a relationship: forcibly established by a man who has imposed his laws on his wife, servants, and children, legitimizing his own arbitrariness through his monopoly of property, that power can be tyrannical in character, and those subject to it can freely accept it if they have "never accustomed to any government before". However, when something changes, when the head of the family dies, and another man takes his place and rules through laws of his own, that power can be questioned. Insofar as it constitutes a deviation from the ordinary social exchange, the novelty may be rejected by those who, though subjected, nevertheless retain their freedom: servants and children begin to murmur, factions and revolts are created, property is dissolved (Cavendish, 1655: 47). In this way, Cavendish brings the lexicon of tyranny and rebellion into the private family, making clear its political character and the risk of the dissolution of one of the gears of the Commonwealth. At this point, women's freedom is no longer simply a possibility inscribed in nature and its movement, but a reasonable political recommendation: a wise husband will have to rule with moderation, "for Kindness melts hardest Hearts, and makes Them flexible to form Them as They please" (Cavendish, 1655: 83).

Cavendish takes her reflection to the extreme consequences only in literary fiction and in particular in *Bell in Campo*, where weak and therefore subordinate women transform themselves and their nature through the discipline of war and military art, and manage to impose themselves on the enemy, as well as on the men who made them slaves, by conquering their freedom (Cavendish, 1999 [1662]).[28] This is not a revolution, but only a "reform", which is manifested primarily in the abolition of coverture, the institution that gave men the exclusive monopoly of property and therefore, in fact, the ability to exercise over women, deprived of any legal personality, a tyrannical rule.[29] Although she does not expressly question the political order based on the subordination of women, which she rather invokes as a necessity against the exorbitant claims of enthusiasts and sectarians, Cavendish points to the cleavage that persists within the representative unit and the possibility of a transformation of its patriarchal structure. Moreover, the novelty she purports to embody would not have been possible without the freedom practiced during the Civil War by women who had spoken publicly, thus invading conventionally male spaces, or who for the first time, like her, had been able to independently exercise certain civil rights in representation of their exiled husbands.[30] All of these were unexpected actions from the patriarchal order. They actually put society in motion

---

28   On Cavendish's *Bell in Campo* see Rudan, 2016.
29   About coverture, see Erickson, 1993.
30   Cf. Chalmers, 2009 [1997].

and polemically activate the concept of woman in history against the masculine claim to immobilize women by defining their nature once and for all.

3   On the Brink of Subversion

In 1700, a different order reigned in England than the one defended by the Duchess of Newcastle. The quiet revolution, which some considered Glorious, left behind the events that turned the country upside down a few decades earlier. The Whig version announced itself as the new historiographical and constitutional canon. John Locke's rationally moral and naturally free individual is established as the undisputed protagonist of modern political discourse. All well and good for some, but evidently not for all. Mary Astell, for example, shows the incongruity of that discourse by formulating a simple question: "if all Men are born free, how is it that all Women are born slaves?" (Astell, 1996 [1706]: 19).[31]

These words have a twofold purpose: first, to support the dynastic legitimacy of Queen Anne Stuart against the destabilizing thrusts of the dissenting doctrine that, from revolution to revolution, had been accommodated to the new constitutional order by keeping open the possibility of overthrowing, in the name of freedom, any government deemed unjust.[32] Secondly, to intervene polemically in the *querelle des femmes* reactivated by the misogynistic satire on marriage.[33] Astell thus speaks in defense of the order, but that order does not provide that she, as a woman, can speak, especially on matters of political importance. It is in fact an order in which men, to guarantee their power, claim to say what a "real woman" is and through this definition to justify her confinement in private space, to indicate the behaviors considered most appropriate to her position, even to establish in the name of God the natural attributes that should oblige every woman to accept those behaviors and this position as a destiny (Astell, 1996 [1706]: 30).

While asserting an unquestionable principle of authority against the doctrine of government by consent, therefore, Astell denounces the unacceptable condition of women's oppression and practically challenges it by speaking out. Her speech is contradictorily articulated between the theological-political

---

31   On Astell's critique of Locke's political thought, see, among others, Springborg, 2005: ch. 3 and Goldie, 2007.

32   Cf. Pocock, 1980.

33   Cf. Lister, 2004 and Perry, 1990.

level[34] – the affirmation of a principle of authority that establishes the radical equality of all who are subject to it – and a worldly and therefore historical understanding of hierarchies and power. Contesting the male definition of what a woman is, this single woman – who was never the daughter of a father, the wife of a husband, the mother of a son[35] – makes sexual difference the perspective from which to speak the truth about order, while she formulates the proposal of a viable change and moves on the brink of a possible subversion.

Astell opens the long 1706 Preface to the second edition of *Some Reflections Upon Marriage* with a gesture that simultaneously conceals her name and reveals her sex. The first operation is necessary to make way for one's arguments, which will have a greater chance of passing "while the Speaker is Incognito". Indeed, these arguments are "Bold Truths", which are difficult to endure because they contradict "the Principles and Practices" of those who hear them, and thus may arouse in them a feeling of enmity toward those who support them. Like Cavendish, Astell thus affirms the novelty of her speaking out and manifests her political intent: "the Reflector ... hopes Reflector is not bad English, now Governor is happily of the Feminine Gender" (Astell, 1996 [1706]: 7–9). The reference to a possible incorrect use of the English language is noteworthy, because the term Reflector has nothing incorrect about it, at least not grammatically. Rather, what is incorrect is the fact that it is a woman who reflects, occupying a position of authority that common language – the expression of established principles and practices – does not allow for any declensions in the feminine form. However, if it were true that women are inferior by nature, as men believe, not only could she herself not speak about science and politics, but no woman would have the right to govern. The association made by Astell between herself as an author and Queen Anne Stuart is therefore of supreme importance: the need to legitimize her own speaking out as a woman goes hand in hand with the need to uphold the legitimacy of the woman sitting on the throne against those who deny the queen's merits because of their envy of her sex, and thus jeopardize "the Liberties not of this or that Nation or Region only, but of the Moiety of Mankind!" (Astell, 1996 [1706]: 31). By speaking out as a woman, Astell thus asserts a perspective that allows her to access a universal truth regarding the principle of authority, as well as the relationship between freedom and obligation. The clash between truth and prejudice

---

34   On the 'antipatriarchal' character of Astell's political theology, which breaks the unity of the theological-political discourse with the affirmation of a subjectivity not admitted to the sacred speech and political power, see the important work of Eleonora Cappuccilli, 2020.

35   About Astell's life and work, see Perry, 1986.

shifts to the relationship between the sexes, which is inevitably charged with a polemical content: "perhaps I've said more than most Men will thank me for, I cannot help it, for how much soever I may be their Friend and Humble Servant, I am more a Friend to Truth" (Astell, 1996 [1700]: 78).[36]

The battlefield defined by Astell evokes the scenario sketched by Nietzsche two centuries later, when he assumes "that truth is a woman" and asks, "why not? Aren't there reasons for suspecting that all philosophers, to the extent that they have been dogmatists, have not really understood women?" (Nietzsche, 2002 [1886]: 3). Actually, according to the philosophers with whom Astell polemicizes, "the natural inferiority" of women can be considered as "a self-evident truth", which as such does not need to be demonstrated and is "fundamental", since an entire system of order is established on it (Astell, 1996 [1706]: 9). Against this dogmatism, the fact that the one who reflects is a woman determines a privileged viewpoint, a condition that is "happy" because it allows access to a deeper degree of knowledge. In support of this conviction, Astell cites Malebranche (Malebranche, 1700: 100), an "extraordinary Genius" whose merit is to have established a clear distinction between knowledge and learning. This distinction, together with the assumption that God had impartially endowed both sexes with the same senses, allows her to affirm that the most exposed to prejudice are men, precisely because they have developed their intellect through education and therefore "will not take the trouble of examining what is contrary to their receiv'd Doctrines". Women and children, on the contrary, "do not dare to judge without examination" (Astell, 1996 [1706]: 21–22).[37] Their association, therefore, does not establish a common condition of minority, but allows for the assertion of an epistemological advantage: if truth is not a received doctrine but the fruit of rational inquiry, then she who has no opinion to defend by force of prejudice will be more willing to seek and thus find truth. The "self-evident" character of women's natural inferiority is something that Astell's own speaking out, like the position occupied by the woman who rules the kingdom, requires one to doubt. What is presented as a natural fact contradicts the equality of the sexes established by God and must therefore be "prov'd" putting each person in a position to judge for himself or herself with his or her own intellect. Woman's truth expresses a radical critique of masculine authority, a critique which presupposes and claims egalitarian possibilities of access to knowledge by questioning the historical conditions that produce sexual difference as subordination (Astell, 1996 [1706]: 10).

---

36   Cf. Kolbrener, 2003: 9 ff.
37   Cf. Board, 2015.

The intellectual superiority of men over women does not depend on their natural constitution, but on custom: "Boys have much Time and Pains, Care and Cost bestow'd on their Education", while "Girls have little or none". The former are encouraged in all ways to devote themselves to science, while the latter are kept away from the "Tree of Knowledge" with all sorts of "Scare-Crows" and when they succeed, despite all the impediments, in escaping ignorance, they are considered "Monsters". If men thus become "Wise and Learned" through years of "Study and Experience", how is it possible to accuse women of not being "Born so"? (Astell, 1996 [1706]: 28). In short, that "the Custom of the World has put Women, generally speaking, into a State of Subjection, is not deny'd; but the Right can no more be prov'd from the Fact, than the Predominancy of Vice can justifie it" (Astell, 1996 [1706]: 10). When custom, or the factual existence of an established and institutionalized social practice, is distinguished from right, then it can be judged, as Astell does by associating it with vice.

The distinction between fact and right allows her working on the level of discourse to show how women's subordination is justified. That is, how the male definition of what a woman is transforms an established social practice into a norm that is valid in general, while every "great and good actions" in which women have been protagonists is treated as an exception that confirms the rule. This is not surprising, if it is true that "Men are the Historians" (Astell, 1717 [1705]: 207): the male monopoly of discourse, and therefore of knowledge, that operates in the masculine signification of the concept of woman, is the expression of a power relationship that must be revealed against any attempt to treat the subordination of women as a natural fact. It is this historical and polemical perspective that guides Astell in her biblical exegesis, which is expressly recognized as a terrain of confrontation with men because, "when an adversary is drove to a Nonplus and Reason declares against him, he flies to Authority, especially to Divine, which is infallible and therefore ought not to be disputed" (Astell, 1996 [1706]: 14). What is questioned, however, is evidently not the divine authority, but the use made of it by those who appeal to it. From the partial perspective of a woman, it is a question of understanding on which side God stands.

The historical reading of Scriptures proposed by Astell focuses on St. Paul's first letter to the Corinthians, where the apostle argues that a woman must cover her head, that she cannot speak, and that she cannot teach within a church. This passage – over which Astell engages in a head-on clash with John Locke[38] – has been used to justify the subordination of women and support

---

38   Specifically, she criticizes Locke, 1987 [1706].

the idea of their intellectual defect as something willed by God and therefore inherently right. In the same letter, however, St. Paul argues that men cannot wear their hair long. Yet, many men in England follow this fashion. We are then faced with a normative problem. If we admit that custom or fashion can alter the Law of Nature and Reason, expression of God's will, then this will would not have the force of law. Otherwise, we must infer that "it is not so much a Law of Nature, that Women shou'd Obey Men, as that Men shou'd not wear long Hair" (Astell, 1996 [1706]: 20, 11–12). St. Paul's text, in short, is nothing more than the expression of the customs of a historical people, and this reading is supported by the fact that he does not speak of women in the plural – indicating the entire female gender – but of woman in the singular, which indicates the wife. Incidentally, it must be remembered that in the etymology of woman there is, in fact, that of 'wife' – *wif* – which does not indicate only a gender difference within the same species (*wif*-man, the human female), but a position within a relationship (the servant of the man).[39] For Astell, therefore, the singular declension of the name does not indicate the generality of sex, but a specific condition, that of the married woman, which is historically characterized by subordination. From this, however, there does not derive any universal norm. Since custom is a fact, which finds linguistic expression in the identification between woman and wife, no right can be legitimately deduced from it.

It is always possible to show the variable and contingent character of custom, and Astell always does this by reading the Scriptures. More precisely, these are invoked against custom: that is, it is a question of searching among the sacred texts for passages that are in favor of women, which therefore escape customs and prejudices – to which the majority of texts give voice by speaking "in the vulgar Mode of Speech", that is, in the common language in which those customs and prejudices are reflected – and can therefore be addressed with "Philosophical Strikness". The instances in which women are actually treated "very differently from what they appear in the common Prejudices of Mankind" (Astell, 1996 [1706]: 22–23) are numerous: Ruth, Esther, Deborah, Miriam are women to whom God revealed himself, granted the gift of prophecy and the office of domestic and civil government, while the Virgin Mary is the one who gave Christ his humanity (Astell, 1996 [1706]: 23–26). Women therefore are not naturally subordinated to men, nor vice versa, but men and women are equal before God,

---

39   Oxford English Dictionary: entry *woman*; cf. Økland, 2004: 14.

> Because GOD made all Things for Himself, and a Rational Mind is too
> noble a Being to be Made for the Sake and Service of any Creature. The
> Service she at any time becomes oblig'd to pay to a Man, is only a Business
> by the Bye.
>
> ASTELL, 1996 [1706]: 11

The equality of the sexes – which Cavendish deduces from their participation
in a common natural substance – for Astell comes from the fact that both
are ultimately dependent on God (Astell, 1996 [1706]: 13). The subjection of
women – like that of the subjects in relation with the sovereign – has no divine
justification, but depends on the secular history inaugurated by sin, because
of which the path of reason was abandoned, and "brutal power" prevailed in
a "struggle for domination". In this struggle women have lost: they have been
subjugated because of their lesser physical strength, and they have been com-
manded to obey in order to obtain quiet, security, and the possibility of exercising virtue. Indeed, there would be no society – whether empires or private
families – without a "last Resort" placed in a certain and uncontested position
that determines its affairs with an "irresistible Sentence". This does not mean,
however, that "Domestic Governors have more Sense than their Subjects, any
more than that other Governors have" (Astell, 1996 [1706]: 15). Like Hobbes,
Astell does not believe that there is any natural basis for rule, but that only
the absolute disorder of the world prescribes an equally absolute and stable
authority, without which the right of the fittest would apply and those without
strength – or the cunning necessary to compensate for their physical weakness – would be doomed to succumb.

Unlike Hobbes, however, Astell does not need to resort to the fiction of the
contract to justify the necessity of obedience and the absoluteness of authority. On the contrary, the very analogy between the subjection of women to
their husbands and that of subjects to the sovereign[40] allows her to explicitly
acknowledge what Hobbes knows well, but only makes explicit in the conclusions of *Leviathan* (Hobbes, 1985 [1651]: 719 ff): that all power is instituted by an
act of force, while all subjection is the result of defeat. The truth of order, seen
from the side of the defeated, is nothing more than "the brutal power" of those
who exercise domination.

Thus, it happened that, while all men were born free, all women became
slaves. Even the Lockean fiction of natural equality, another important moment
in the gestation process of modern politics, thus conceals an act of power, the

---

40   On this analogy, see Weiss, 2016.

unspoken secret of the rational and free individual who is its protagonist. Once this secret is revealed, the fact of masculine domination becomes for Astell the lever to challenge the logic of government by consent, from which the idea that sovereignty must be limited derives. The question that made her famous is thus introduced by these words:

> If Absolute Sovereignty be not necessary in a State, how comes it to be so in a Family? Or if in a Family why not in a State; since no Reason can be alledg'd for the one that will not hold more strongly for the other? ... The Domestic Sovereign is without Dispute Elected, and the Stipulations and Contract are mutual, is it not then partial in Men to the last degree, to contend for, and practice that Arbitrary Dominion in their Families, which they abhor and exclaim against in the State?
>
> ASTELL, 1996 [1706]: 19

Astell's pressing questions express her immediately political intent, linked to the events of which she is a spectator. The aim is to affirm the principle of dynastic legitimacy embodied by Anne Stuart and the absolute character of her sovereignty against Lockean contractualism, that is, against the persistence of the dissenting doctrine which, by bringing William of Orange to the throne, had interrupted that continuity and caused the stability of the monarchical order to waver. The effects of his stringent logic, however, go beyond the vicissitudes of the kingdom and raise a question which is unthinkable in terms of Locke's discourse: that of power as a presupposition – and not simply an effect – of the contract. Marriage, from this point of view, is exemplary: precisely because it is a contract, it can be said that the husband, the domestic sovereign, is chosen by the woman, whose consent, however, does not express any freedom: "a Woman indeed can't propertly be said to Choose", when she has been taught all her life that her highest design is to have a husband (Astell, 1996 [1700]: 43, 65–66). For Astell, it is not possible to think of the individual in abstraction from the power relations within which he or she finds him or herself acting and expressing consent. The fact of masculine domination founds law, as well as custom, and survives within them by determining their cogency.

Marriage, therefore, is the institutional form of sexual subjugation, and in fact at the very moment a woman marries a man "she puts her self intirely in his Power, leaves all that is dear to her ... to espouse his interests ... and makes it her Business and Duty to please him" (Astell, 1996 [1706]: 55). Masculine domination explains why even a man who condemns arbitrary power when it sits on the throne "wou'd cry up Liberty to poor Female Slaves of plead for

the Lawfulness of Resisting a Private Tyranny", lest he see his own supremacy challenged (Astell, 1996 [1706]: 46–47). The condition of the woman in
marriage is therefore a condition of slavery, yet for Astell it has a precise function of order: to reproduce the species in an honorable way and ensure the
education of children, the transmission of the paternal name, the continuity
of the family and property. All this means toil and trouble for women, who
nevertheless must fulfill these duties as what is necessary to maintain order,
if the alternative is an all-out struggle for domination and the right of the
strongest. Therefore, marriage is justified by society and protected by civil law.
Above all, it is a sacred Christian institution, in which obedience to the worst
of tyrants is not only necessary in the interest of order, but also evidence of
love for God and the nobility of the soul of those who submit (Astell, 1996
[1706]: 36–7, 58).

However, precisely for the sake of God and order, even if they find themselves
in subjection, even if they are placed under the yoke of a man who has "usurp'd
an Empire over [their] Understandings", women can exercise their own faculties of judgment and oppose the follies of their husbands when these call into
question the obedience due to governors. While not justifying insubordination
to the domestic tyrant, Astell acknowledges an inner freedom for women that
they can and must practice in order to live up to their Christian duty. Obedience
to worldly authority must not be blind, but in accordance with reason (Astell,
1717 [1705]: 31–2). In this conscious subjection – in this duty for duty's sake that
anticipates the Kantian imperative by showing its effects of domination – what
is expressed is the freedom of the mind, something that not even the most absolute of tyrants can touch (Astell, 1996 [1700]: 75, 56). Precisely within a tyrannical marriage, then, "Affliction [is] the sincerest friend, the frankest Monitor, the
best Instructer, and indeed the only useful School that Women are ever put to",
since it "rouses her understanding, opens her Eyes, fixes her Attention", allowing
one to distinguish between truth and appearance (Astell, 1996 [1700]: 40). As in
Pizan, marriage is the site of a martyrdom that allows women to exercise their
Christian virtues to the fullest.

Astell's political theology thus marks both the beginning and the limit of
her discourse: by postulating the equality of men and women before God, it is
charged with an antipatriarchal valence that allows her to contest masculine
domination as a historical rather than a natural fact, and to criticize its institutionalization within marriage. The latter, however, remains a Christian institution that cannot be criticized to the core without questioning God's authority
that guarantees the equality of souls. Political theology ultimately proves to be
a trap because it articulates a discourse on possible freedom from a principle

of necessary order.[41] Although it allows women to be thought of as equal, God is not on their side.

Because of the limitations that divine authority imposes on her critique, Astell makes some reasonable suggestions geared toward improving the status of married women, and these suggestions bring her closer to Cavendish, though the latter articulates them from premises grounded in the immanence of nature and its historical movements, rather than theological-political ones. To the extent that it is inspired by the love of God, domestic government can and should be wisely administered in his name and for the good of those in subjection, rather than in the private interest of those in worldly authority. Under these conditions, a wife will obey not out of necessity but according to reason, leaving her husband's dominion over this world in the knowledge that there will come a time – the time of salvation – when "her Sex shall be no bar to the best Employments, the highest Honour" (Astell, 1996 [1700]: 75). However, since "a wise Man and a Husband are not Terms convertible" (Astell, 1996 [1700]: 62), it must be admitted that the tyrannical exercise of masculine domination can expose the institution of marriage to insubordination. Women are, "for the most part, Wise enough to Love their Chains, and to discern how very becomingly they set" (Astell, 1996 [1700]: 29), but the episode of the Duchess of Mazzarino – one of the pretexts that determined the writing of the *Reflections* – demonstrates that they might seek satisfaction in companionship or seduction rather than submitting to their private tyrants (Astell, 1996 [1700]: 26-9, 31-3).

Astell does not justify this behavior, but basically understands it, or at least takes note of it: "I don't say that Tyranny ought, but we find in Fact that it provokes the Oppress'd to throw off even a lawful Yoke that fits too heavy" (Astell, 1996 [1700]: 78). Without prejudice to the distinction between fact and right, rebellion becomes a possibility that is actually viable if those who are subjugated are "Strong enough to break the Yoke" (Astell, 1996 [1700]: 46-47). In the case of women this is unlikely, because they "are not so well united as to form an Insurrection", but history itself – even the most recent history of England – teaches that it is possible (Astell 1996 [1700]: 29).[42] Thus, if Astell's political theology requires her to recognize the existence of hierarchies as a necessary condition for the establishment of order, her entirely worldly reading of domination allows her to point to the concrete possibility of change.

---

41   On the coexistence of equality and hierarchy in Astell's thinking see Bejan 2019. On the relationship between theology and politics, see Galli 2018.

42   In *Moderation Truly Stated* Astell refers to the abilities of leadership displayed by dissenting women (Astell, 1704: xlix).

This possibility can be practiced by each individual woman starting from
the awareness that under existing historical conditions, when she "Elects a
Monarch for Life" and gives him "an Authority she cannot recall, ... puts her
Fortune and Person entirely in his Powers" (Astell, 1996 [1700]: 48). Since there
is no security in trusting in the good nature of the man to whom she gives herself completely, a woman will have to rely on herself and "think twice" before
marrying (Astell, 1996 [1700]: 49). This means, first of all, not to give in to flattery: he who in courtship declares himself a slave of love does so with the sole
purpose of enslaving a woman for life. Exercise diffidence, therefore, but also
a sense of honor, preserving one's reputation and behaving with moderation
and discretion, caution, and foresight (Astell, 1996 [1700]: 51). Astell knows that
this cautious attitude and self-discipline might turn women away from marriage; she foresees this possibility and tries to downplay it in the eyes of her
male readers, stating that ultimately her intent is only to show women how
to distinguish between a man capable of being a wise husband and one destined to become a domestic tyrant (Astell, 1996 [1700]: 49, 45, 73–74, 77–80).
However, when she speaks to the female reader – to whom, changing register,
she addresses by calling her "you" – she becomes an advocate of a freedom that
is practicable even against marriage, which does not question the subordination of the wife because it takes place before her subjection and on another
stage. Women, in other words, can choose not to marry, so that self-discipline
becomes a way to determine their own position outside of the customs that
determine their oppression. This is certainly not easy, in a world where masculine domination is embedded in law and coverture prevents women from
disposing of their own property, while even those without fathers or husbands
are placed under guardianship (Astell, 1996 [1706]: 29). Still, escaping marriage
is a viable option, and Astell actually practiced it. Her *Serious Proposal to the
Ladies*, the project of a secular "monastery" for women which she had only
given to the press a few years before, is the premise and support of that possibility, which certainly does not indicate the subversion of the main institution
of masculine domination, but at least the opportunity that every single woman
can take to escape from its grip and defeat "the tyranny of custom" (Astell,
2002 [1694–1697]: 69).[43] As wives, women must be subordinate, but there is
nothing to prevent them from occupying a different place in the earthly hierarchy from the one that masculine domination provides for them. The case of
Queen Anne shows that "if by Custom or Contract, or the Laws of the Country,
or Birth Right ... they have the supreme Authority, it is no Usurpation" (Astell,

---

43   About the *Serious Proposal* see Smith, 2007; Sowaal, 2007.

1996 [1700]: 26). The concept of woman is not the signifier of a condition of subordination that is ontologically based and therefore immutable, but the result of a process of signification wherein what is expressed is the cogency of laws and customs which, as historical facts, are unstable and exposed to change. The woman's truth, the struggle for a definition of herself and her position against that imposed by masculine domination, shows that this domination is only "a Business by the bye", that is, incidental. Astell is not a subversive, but her search for truth points to a possibility that many women at the turn of the century would have practiced collectively by claiming, in the name of their sex, a revolution.

References

Ankers, N. (2003) Paradigms and Politics: Hobbes and Cavendish Contrasted. In: Clucas S. (ed) *A Princely Brave Woman. Essays on Margaret Cavendish, Duchess of Newcastle.* Aldershot: Ashgate, 242–254.

Astell, M. (1704) *Moderation Truly Stated.* London: R. Wilkin.

Astell, M. (1717 [1705]) *The Christian Religion as Profess'd by a Daughter of the Church of England.* London: E. Wilkin.

Astell, M. (1996 [1700]) Some Reflections upon Marriage. In: Astell M. (1996) *Political Writings.* Springborg P. (ed). Cambridge: Cambridge University Press, 32–80.

Astell, M. (1996 [1706]) Preface to Reflections upon Marriage. In: Astell M. (1996) *Political Writings.* Springborg P. (ed). Cambridge: Cambridge University Press, 1–31.

Astell, M. (2002 [1694–1697]) *A Serious Proposal to the Ladies, Parts I and II.* Springborg P. (ed). Peterborough: Broadview Press.

Augustine (2008 [413]) *The City of God Books VIII–XVI.* Walsh G.G. and Monahan G. (eds). Washington: The Catholic University of America Press.

Augustine (2003 [422–426]) *On the Trinity Books 8–15.* Matthews G.B. and McKenna S. (eds). Cambridge: Cambridge University Press.

Bejan, T.M. (2019) "Since All the World is Mad, Why Should Not I Be So"? Mary Astell on Equality, Hierarchy, and Ambition. *Political Theory* 47/6: 781–808.

Board, J. (2015) *The Philosophy of Mary Astell: An Early Modern Theory of Virtue.* Oxford: Oxford University Press.

Bock, G. (2002) *Women in European History.* Oxford: Blackwell Publishing.

Boethius (2008 [c.524]) *The Consolation of Philosophy.* Slavitt D.R. and Lerer S. (eds). Cambridge (MS) – London: Harvard University Press.

Bonasera, J. (2019) "Il sedizioso muggito di una nazione turbata". Malinconici e profeti nel pensiero politico di Thomas Hobbes. *Filosofia Politica* 1: 137–152.

Cappuccilli, E. (2015) Remarkable Women in a Remarkable Age. Sulla genesi della sfera pubblica inglese, 1642–1752. *Scienza & Politica. Per una storia delle dottrine* 52: 105–134.

Cappuccilli, E. (2020) *La critica imprevista. Politica, teologia e patriarcato in Mary Astell.* Macerata: EUM.

Carrol, B.A. (1998) Christine de Pizan and the Origins of Peace Theory. In: Smith H.L. (ed) *Women Writers and the Early Modern British Political Tradition.* Cambridge: Cambridge University Press, 22–39.

Cavendish, M. (1655) *The World's Olio.* London: J. Martin and J. Allestrye.

Cavendish, M. (1662) *Orations of Divers Sorts, Accommodated to Divers Places. Written by the Thrice Noble, Illustrious and Excellent Princess, the Lady Marchioness of Newcastle.* London: s.p.

Cavendish, M. (1664) *Philosophical Letters.* London: s.p.

Cavendish, M. (1999 [1662]) Bell in Campo. In: Cavendish M. (1999) *The Convent of Pleasure and Other Plays.* Shaver A. (ed). Baltimore: The John Hopkins University Press, 107–169.

Cavendish, M. (2003 [1666]) The Description of a New World, Called the Blazing World. In: James, S. (ed) *Margaret Cavendish. Political Writings.* Cambridge: Cambridge University Press, 3–109.

Chalmers, H. (2009 [1997]) Dismantling the Myth of "Mad Madge": The Cultural Context of Margaret Cavendish Authorial Self-Presentation. In: Mendelson S.H. (ed) *Ashgate Critical Essays on Women Writers in England, 1550–1700. Vol. 7, Margaret Cavendish.* Farnham: Ashgate, 35–54.

Col, G. (2007 [1401]) Gontier Col's Reply to Christine de Pizan after She Had Sent Him a Copy of Her Letter to Jean de Montreuil. In: McWebb C. (ed) *Debating the Roman de la Rose. A Critical Anthology.* New York – London: Routledge, 134–135.

Col, P. (2007 [1402]) Reply to Christine de Pizan's and Jean Gerson's Treatises. In: McWebb C. (ed) *Debating the Roman de la Rose. A Critical Anthology.* New York-London: Routledge, 306–343.

Descartes, R. (2006 [1637]) *A Discourse on the Method of Correctly Conducting One's Reason and Seeking Truth in the Sciences.* Maclean I. (ed). Oxford: Oxford University Press.

Duso, G. (1999) *La logica del potere. Storia concettuale come filosofia politica.* Roma – Bari: Laterza.

Erickson, A.L. (1993) *Women and Property in Early Modern England.* London – New York: Routledge.

Falleiros, B. (2010) Fortune, force d'ordre ou de désordre chez Christine de Pizan. *Camenulae* 5. Available (consulted 22 April 2023) at: https://www.academia.edu/8430 527/Fortune_force_dordre_ou_de_d%C3%A9sordre_chez_Christine_de_Pizan.

Galli, C. (2009) *Contingenza e necessità nella ragione politica moderna*. Roma – Bari: Laterza.

Galli, C. (2011) All'insegna del Leviatano. Potere e destino del progetto politico moderno. In: Hobbes T. *Il Leviatano*. Milano: BUR, V–L.

Galli, C. (2018) Teologia politica: strutture e critica. In: Stimilli E. (ed) *Teologie e politica*, Macerata: Quodlibet, 29–51.

Gentili, A. (1993 [1612]) *De iure belli libris tres*. Oxford: Clarendon Press.

Goldie, M. (2007) Mary Astell and John Locke. In: Kolbrener W. and Michelson M. (eds) *Mary Astell. Reason, Gender, Faith*. Aldershot: Ashgate, 65–85.

Green, K. (1994) Christine De Pisan and Thomas Hobbes. *The Philosophical Quarterly* 177: 456–475.

Hicks, E. (1977) La querelle de la Rose dans la pensée historique. In: Hicks E. (ed) *Le Débat sur le Roman de la Rose*. Paris: Éditions Honoré Champion, IX–XCIX.

Hicks, E., Gonzalez, D. and Simon, P. (2000) *Au champ des escriptures. IIIe Colloque international sur Christine de Pizan*. Paris: Honoré Champion.

Hobbes, T. (1985 [1651]) *Leviathan*. MacPherson C.B. (ed). London: Penguin.

Hobbes, T. (1987 [1642]) *De Cive. The English Version*. Warrender H. (ed). Oxford: Clarendon Press.

Kelly, D. (2007) *Christine de Pizan's Changing Opinion. A Quest for Certainty in the Midst of Chaos*. Cambridge: D.S. Brewer.

Kelly, J. (1982) Early Feminist Theory and the Querelle des Femmes, 1400–1789. *Signs* 1: 4–28.

Kennedy, A.J. (1984) *Christine de Pizan: A Bibliographical Guide*. London: Grant and Cutler.

Kolbrener, W. (2003) Gendering the Modern: Mary Astell's Feminist Historiography. *The Eighteenth Century* 1: 1–24.

Koselleck, R. (2004 [1979]) *Futures Past. On the Semantics of Historical Time*. New York: Columbia University Press.

Langdon Forhan, K. (2002) *The Political Theory of Christine de Pizan*. London and New York: Routledge.

Lilley, K. (2003) Contracting Readers: "Margaret Newcastle" and the Rhetoric of Conjugality. In: Clucas S. (ed) *A Princely Brave Woman. Essays on Margaret Cavendish, Duchess of Newcastle*. Aldershot: Ashgate, 19–39.

Lister, A. (2004) Marriage and Misogyny: The Place of Mary Astell in the History of Political Thought. *History of Political Thought* 1: 44–72.

Locke, J. (1987 [1706]) *A Paraphrase and Notes on the Epistles of St Paul*. Wainwright A.W. (ed). Oxford: Clarendon Press.

Lorris, G. de and Meun, J. de (1995 [1237–1280]) *The Romance of the Rose*. Princeton (NJ): Princeton University Press.

Machiavelli, N. (2008 [1513–1514]) *The Prince*. Atkinson J.B. (ed). Indianapolis – Cambridge: Hackett Publishing Company.

Malcolmson, C. (2002) Christine de Pizan's City of Ladies in Early Modern England. In: Malcolmson C. and Suzuki M. (eds) *Debating Gender in Early Modern England, 1500–1700*. New York: Palgrave Macmillan, 15–36.

Malebranche, N. (1700) *Father Malebranche His Treatise Concerning the Search After Truth*. London: Thomas Bennet *et. al.*

Montreuil, J. de (2007 [1402]) Epistle 154. In: McWebb C. (ed) *Debating the Roman de la Rose. A Critical Anthology*. New York – London: Routledge, 344–347.

Muzzarelli, M.G. (2007) *Un'italiana alla corte di Francia: Christine de Pizan, intellettuale e donna*. Bologna: Il Mulino.

Nicolosi, M.G. (2008) Introduzione. In: Cavendish M. *Il mondo sfavillante*. Catania: c.u.e.c.m., 7–104.

Nietzsche, F. (2002 [1886]) *Beyond Good and Evil*. Horstmann R.-P. and Norman J. (eds). Cambridge: Cambridge University Press.

Økland, J. (2004) *Women in Their Place: Paul and the Corinthian Discourse of Gender and Sanctuary Space*. London – New York: T&T Clark International.

Opitz, C. (2017) La vita quotidiana delle donne nel tardo medioevo (1250–1500). Klapisch-Zuber, Ch. (ed) *Storia delle donne. Il medioevo*. Roma – Bari: Laterza, 330–401.

Pateman, C. (1988) *The Sexual Contract*. Stanford: Stanford University Press.

Perry, R. (1986) *The Celebrated Mary Astell. An Early English Feminist*. Chicago – London: The University of Chicago Press.

Perry, R. (1990) Mary Astell and the Feminist Critique of Possessive Individualism. *Eighteenth-Century Studies* 4: 444–457.

Peterman, A. (2019) Margaret Cavendish on Motion and Mereology. *Journal of the History of Philosophy* 3: 471–499.

Piccinini, M. (2007) *Corpo politico, opinione pubblica, società politica. Per una storia dell'idea inglese di Costituzione*. Torino: Giappichelli.

Pitkin, H.F. (1999) *Fortune is a Woman. Gender & Politics in the Thought of Niccolò Machiavelli*. Chicago – London: Chicago University Press.

Pizan, C. de (1982 [1405]) *The Book of the City of Ladies*. New York: Persea Books.

Pizan, C. de (2007 [1401]) Christine's Reaction to Jean de Montreuil's Treatise on the Roman de la rose. In: McWebb C. (ed) *Debating the Roman de la Rose. A Critical Anthology*. New York – London: Routledge, 118–133.

Pizan, C. de (2007 [1402a]) Letter to the Queen Isabeau de Bavière. In: McWebb C. (ed) *Debating the Roman de la Rose. A Critical Anthology*. New York – London: Routledge, 108–111.

Pizan, C. de (2007 [1402b]) Christine's Epistle to Guillaume de Tignonville. In: McWebb C. (ed) *Debating the Roman de la Rose. A Critical Anthology*. New York – London: Routledge, 216–218.

Pizan, C. de (2007 [1402c]) Christine's Response to Pierre Col. In: McWebb C. (ed) *Debating the Roman de la Rose. A Critical Anthology*. New York – London: Routledge, 140–189.

Pizan, C. de (2017 [1403]) *The Book of the Mutability of Fortune*. Toronto, Ontario: Iter Press.

Pizan, C. de (1998 [1406–1407]) *Le livre du corps de policie*. Kennedy A.G. (ed). Paris: Champion.

Pocock, J.G.A. (1980) *Three British Revolutions: 1641, 1688, 1776*. Princeton: Princeton University Press.

Rudan, P. (2015) "Tanto difficili da comprendere quanto l'universo". Margaret Cavendish e l'arte sessuale della retorica. *Filosofia politica* 29: 251–260.

Rudan, P. (2016) Riscrivere la storia, fare la storia. Sulla donna come soggetto in Christine de Pizan e Margaret Cavendish. *Scienza & Politica. Per una storia delle dottrine* 54: 21–41.

Rudan, P. (2020) Una distanza civile e politica. Master Hobbes e Margaret Cavendish. In: Lanzillo M.L. and Laudani R. (eds) *Figure del potere. Saggi in onore di Carlo Galli*. Bologna: Il Mulino: 163–179.

Sarasohn, L.T. (2010) *The Natural Philosophy of Margaret Cavendish: Reason and Fancy during the Scientific Revolution*. Baltimore: The John Hopkins University Press.

Schochet, G.J. (1967) Thomas Hobbes on the Family and the State of Nature. *Political Science Quarterly* 3: 427–445.

Shahar, S. (2003) *The Fourth Estate. A History of Women in the Middle Ages*. London – New York: Routledge.

Siegfried, B.R. and Sarasohn, L.T. (2014) *God and Nature in the Thought of Margaret Cavendish*. Farnham: Ashgate.

Smith, H. (2007) Mary Astell, *A Serious Proposal to the Ladies* (1694), *and the Anglican Reformation of Manners in Late Seventeenth-Century England*. In: Kolbrener W. and Michelson M. (eds) *Mary Astell. Reason, Gender, Faith*. Aldershot: Ashgate, 31–47.

Sowaal, A. (2007) Mary Astell's Serious Proposal: Mind, Method, and Custom. *Philosophy Compass* 2: 227–243.

Springborg, P. (2005) *Mary Astell. Theorist of Freedom from Domination*. Cambridge: Cambridge University Press.

Van Engen, J. (2008) Multiple Options: The World of the Fifteenth-Century Church. *Church History* 2: 257–284.

Walters, L. (2014) *Margaret Cavendish. Gender, Science and Politics*. Cambridge: Cambridge University Press.

Walters, L.J. (2000) La Réécriture de Saint Augustin par Christine de Pizan: de la *Cité de Dieu* à la *Cité des Dames*. In: Hicks E., Gonzalez D. and Simon P. (eds) *Au champ des escriptures. IIIe Colloque international sur Christine de Pizan.* Paris: Honoré Champion, 197–215.

Weiss, P.A. (2016) "From the Throne to Every Private Family". Mary Astell as Analyst of Power. In: Sowaal A. and Weiss P.A. (eds) *Feminist Interpretations of Mary Astell.* University Park (PA): Penn State University Press, 128–152.

Whitaker, K. (2004) *Mad Madge. Margaret Cavendish, Duchess of Newcastle, Royalist, Writer & Romantic.* London: Vintage.

Willard, C.C. (1984) *Christine de Pizan: Her Life and Works.* New York: Persea Books.

Zimmermann, M. and De Rentiis, D. (1994) *The City of Scholars. New Approaches to Christine de Pizan,* 2 vols. Berlin – New York: Walter de Gruyter.

CHAPTER 2

The Social Production of Difference

1   The Woman and the Others

In *Reflections on the Revolution in France*, Edmund Burke describes the morning of October 6, 1789, when an army of "furies of hell in the abused shape of the vilest of women" forced Louis XVI and Marie Antoinette to flee the palace of Versailles. The tones manifest his contempt: taking to the streets, abandoning the demeanor prescribed to their sex, the *sans culottes* offer striking evidence of revolutionary excesses. To their degradation, Burke contrasts the "delightful vision" of Marie Antoinette, who demonstrates what a true woman should be (Burke, 1999 [1790]: 165, 169).[1] In addition to discrediting the revolutionaries, he thus reaffirmed the legitimacy of the monarchy by opposing every democratic claim made by the mob: the women of the vulgar, the workers, the poor and all the figures to whom the Revolution had opened an unprecedented space for action. In this space, women appeared as a social movement that, through the practice of its political discourse, challenged and tormented modern politics. This is the great novelty that the French Revolution clearly announces. From this moment on, feminism takes on a collective form that goes beyond the important philosophical and theological reflections of individual women who had rejected patriarchal rule in previous centuries. Despite the importance of these reflections, the novelty here is not only that women themselves pose the problem of their common action with increasing strength, but also the increasingly clear and problematic awareness that theirs is a mass condition capable of displacing all the political terrains it crosses.

The March for Bread at Versailles and the expulsion of the royal family from the palace shook not only Burke but also the French revolutionaries, who hastened to eclipse the disorder brought by women in history by declaring that man was the only legitimate subject of the political order to which the Revolution gave rise.[2] Yet, the role of women was crucial in forcing the king to sign the *Declaration of the Rights of Man and of the Citizen*, and in fact their response was not long in coming.[3] In 1791, Olympe de Gouges argues that the Revolution has not put an end to ancient privileges, because masculine

---

1   On Burke's conception of femininity, see Zerilli, 1994: ch. 3.
2   Pateman, 2003 [1980]: 17.
3   See Michelet, 1855 [1854]: ch. IV; Godineau, 1988; Viola, 1989: 83–87.

domination continues even in the new time that the Revolution has inaugurated. *The Declaration of the Rights of Woman and the Female Citizen* shows what political stakes are hidden within the silence imposed on women. De Gouges rewrites Article XI of the 1789 *Declaration* in order to also recognize a woman's right to publicly declare who is the father of her child (de Gouges, 1986 [1791]: 104–105). Her freedom to take the stand, her speaking out, threatens the certainty of the paternal transmission of property and name, to the point that the *Code Napoléon* has forbidden the mothers of "bastards" to seek out the natural father of their children. The subordination of women, which continues alongside the bourgeois equality of men and is its presupposition, makes the French Revolution a broken promise, as had already been true for the American Revolution. However, if in the aftermath of independence Abigail Adams had turned to her husband John – a delegate to the Continental Congress in Philadelphia – inviting him to "remember the ladies" (Adams, 1875: 49), de Gouges now turns directly to women, because it is up to them to realize that promise: "fellow citizens, would it not be time that we made a revolution among us?" (de Gouges, 1792: 115).

Precisely because the protagonist quality of women – which had already manifested itself during the English Civil War – is accompanied by a reflection on their position in society, from 1789 onwards the concept of woman is charged with a polemical content, an expectation of freedom and an unprecedented democratic ambition. In the *Sattelzeit*, the concept of woman becomes the indicator of the 'genetic crisis' of the modern political universal, because it expresses the pretension of realizing it by declining it in the feminine singular, and for this reason it manifests the impossibility of doing it without confronting with the political and social conditions of its affirmation. Mary Wollstonecraft's reflection is relevant precisely because, while claiming the rights of woman, she is forced to confront the different positions that society assigns to women. First and foremost, therefore, she brings to light the contradiction between the ambition to make woman the subject of a universal emancipation, which is expressed in the language of rights, and the impossibility that woman embodies a universal, both because of the partiality of which she is necessarily the bearer, and because her position is always and inevitably socially determined.

Wollstonecraft does not fit the neat aristocratic ideal of femininity invoked by Burke: lacking annuity, she worked for a living; she experienced love outside and against marriage and experienced it tragically, pushing herself to the brink of death; she traversed the political scene of her time by becoming a direct observer of the French Revolution. She thought of this event with enthusiasm, though not without concern in the face of the Jacobin Terror; however, she never fully condemned revolutionary violence, seeing it as a reaction of the oppressed to oppression that was, if not justifiable, at least understandable (Wollstonecraft, 2011 [1794]: 13).[4] With a clearsighted understanding of the weight of history on the events of 1789, Wollstonecraft responds to Burke that his "furies of hell" are women who make their living selling vegetables and fish at the market and who have never known the advantages of education. They "have almost insuperable obstacles to surmount in their progress towards true dignity of character" (Wollstonecraft, 2008 [1790]: 29), and their violence is the effect of the ignorance that has governed their actions, of the prejudice and superstition that have infested minds, influenced behavior, and determined the "imperfect" character of the institutions of government and that "hetero-geneous mass" called "the constitution" (Wollstonecraft, 2008 [1790]: 11). Burke does not grasp the novelty and the possibilities opened by the Revolution because he judges them from the past, from a "servile reverence for antiquity", from a cult of the authority of "canonized *forefathers*" that closes the doors to the exercise of reason (Wollstonecraft, 2008 [1790]: 13, 19).[5] The past must be recognized as a burden from which to be freed in the light of the "simple prin-ciples" affirmed by the Revolution, an equality of rights whose full realization concerns the future (Wollstonecraft, 2011 [1794]: 295). This squinting, modern look at the present – stretched between the space of experience and the hori-zon of expectation – announces the contradiction in which Wollstonecraft is caught when she discovers the social process that produces women and denies them access to the equality they claim.

Anticipating by a century and a half Simone de Beauvoir's most famous sentence – "one is not born, but rather becomes, a woman" (Beauvoir, 1956 [1949]: 273) – Wollstonecraft argues that females "were made women, almost from their very birth" (Wollstonecraft, 1792: 21), and in particular from the moment in which education begins to imprint on them a "sexual character" (Wollstonecraft, 2014 [1792]: 109). Woman is an "artificial" being. The adjective appears repeatedly in Wollstonecraft's work as a polemic against those who invoke nature in order to justify the subordination of women as a consequence of their inability to submit their passions to reason. The target here is first of all Rousseau (Wollstonecraft, 2014 [1792]: 51 ff),[6] but clearly also an ancient tradition still active in the Age of Enlightenment. The coquettish, sensual, unreasonable, and passionate woman that patriarchal discourse condemns as

---

4   For a general overview on Wollstonecraft's life and works see Bergés and Coffee, 2016; Casalini, 2008; Gordon, 2005; Todd, 2000.
5   On the debate between Wollstonecraft and Burke, see O'Neill, 2007.
6   On Wollstonecraft and Rousseau cf. Cossutta, 2017.

a minor has nothing natural about her. Her character is artificial, as well as the notions of beauty and sensitivity that have been inculcated since childhood as "motives of action" (Wollstonecraft, 2014 [1792]: 70). Her weakness, the idea of a dependence on man that stems from an improper generalization of her lesser physical strength, is again artificial. The roots of subordination are not to be found in the imperfection of nature, but in civilization: the dependent and irrational woman is the "civilized woman" (Wollstonecraft, 2014 [1792]: 175). Precisely because she challenges any possibility of ontologically justifying the subordination of women, Wollstonecraft must investigate the material conditions under which they come into the world and how those conditions position them within the world.

The civilization that produces woman is unaccomplished, "partial" (Wollstonecraft, 2014 [1792]: 29), because it bears the mark of feudal society. Wollstonecraft makes use of the *Theory of Moral Sentiments*, applying Adam Smith's analysis of the "general character" of the individuals belonging to the highest ranks of society to the female sex (Wollstonecraft, 2014 [1792]: 85).[7] Such ranks do not stand out because of a strength of character derived from the exercise of their faculties or from industry, but because of the admiration held for them by individuals of the lower ranks in whose gaze they are mirrored. Conforming to their expectation, the nobleman replicates through "his air, his manner, his deportment, ... that elegant and graceful sense of his own superiority" conferred upon him by his subordinates (Wollstonecraft, 2014 [1792]: 86). Like the nobleman, women are placed in their rank "by courtesy" and, instead of honing their physical and intellectual strength by giving practical proof of their virtue, they favor appearance over substance and exhibit the patience, docility, good humor, and flexibility expected of them by their suitors (Wollstonecraft, 2014 [1792]: 86). Like the nobleman, the woman also actively participates in this dynamic of social mirroring by virtue of the "love of [the] power" (Wollstonecraft, 2014 [1792]: 54) she can exercise by leveraging the man's desire for pleasure, which exposes him to the flattery of coquetry. While the woman's power of seduction acts in an "oblique" manner, however, the man's remains "predominant" and sets the tone for the entire process of socialization of which the woman is the product (Wollstonecraft, 2014 [1792]: 53, 73). She "was created to be the toy of man"; moralists have lavished all their efforts on making her a docile being and infusing into her bosom a "spaniel-like affection" (Wollstonecraft, 2014 [1792]: 59). Woman, in a word, has been "domesticated" (Wollstonecraft, 2014 [1792]: 91), Wollstonecraft claims, choosing a term

---

7   Cf. Smith, 2002 [1759]: part I, s. 3, ch. 2 and 3; on Wollstonecraft and Smith see Leddy, 2016.

that not only refers to her forced segregation in domestic and private space, but also defines the social process that transforms fact into law and justifies the subordination of woman *a posteriori* as natural, causing this subordination to be accepted even by those it condemns to obedience (Wollstonecraft 2014, [1792]: 73). The *ancien régime* has refined manners at the expense of morality, making even man – and not only woman – into an "artificial monster" fascinated by power instead of friendship, by elegance and taste instead of the beauty that resides in a God-fearing heart (Wollstonecraft, 2008 [1790]: 8–9, 59). Sex, however, diversifies the outcomes of this process: the corruption of civilized society also involves man and not just woman, but only the former benefits.

Wollstonecraft's analogy developed between the dynamics of socialization typical of feudal society and those that produce and legitimize the subordination of women allows her to think of masculine domination as a form of privilege that is reproduced even among the middle ranks, that is, in that commercial society that develops in the bosom of feudal society, carrying the germ of its crisis. The subordination of women, therefore, marks the presence of feudalism within the society of individuals, the constant operation of an 'anachronism' in the progressive time of modernity. While men are driven from their youth to prepare for the professions that they can and must exercise, women are directed towards marriage as if this were the main goal of their existence, the only scheme they have to "sharpen their faculties". Wollstonecraft thus defines marriage as a form of "legal prostitution" (Wollstonecraft, 2014 [1792]: 87) because women from the middle ranks – to whom social conventions deny the possibility of working – are forced to marry in order to support themselves, but also because it constitutes a market space in which they move embellished from one public place to another in order to put themselves on display as matrimonial commodities, in constant competition with other women (Wollstonecraft, 2014 [1792]: 201, 219). Marriage institutionalizes a relationship of domination that persists even when the impersonality of modern sovereignty is affirmed, so much so that Wollstonecraft defines every husband as a despot or tyrant to his wife (Wollstonecraft, 2014 [1792]: 23, 255). As she investigates the historical conditions of its production, Wollstonecraft is forced to recognize that the subordination of woman is the outcome of a specific "constitution of civil society" (Wollstonecraft, 2014 [1792]: 32), that masculine domination in other words is a 'constitutional factor'.[8] Thus, it is not nature

---

8   The formula 'constitutional factor' is used to indicate the elements for a history of the constitution in a material sense. Cf. Schiera, 1986.

that determines woman's inability to act rationally, but society that prevents her "from attaining that sovereignty" which would make her "a rational creature useful to others" (Wollstonecraft, 2014 [1792]: 88). In this way, the rationality that distinguishes the modern individual and makes him sovereign is itself revealed as a privilege:

> We might as well never have been born, unless it were necessary that we should be created to enable man to acquire the noble privilege of reason, the power of discerning good from evil, whilst we lie down in the dust from whence we were taken, never to rise again.
>
> WOLLSTONECRAFT, 2014 [1792]: 89

Bringing the language of tyranny into the domestic sphere, Wollstonecraft vindicates woman's rights against her artificial subordination. In her critique, the theological-political argument for the equality of men and women before God, already present in Astell, is rearticulated in light of the Kantian doctrine of virtue, which does not regard morality as an innate character, but as the practice of relating to others and to oneself through others.[9] Nature may generate physical differences and differences in talents, but these differences – starting with that between the sexes – are irrelevant from a moral point of view and do not justify any relationship of domination (Wollstonecraft, 2014 [1792]: 69). God has conferred on all his creatures without distinction the rights that give them the capacity to be free, that is, the rational faculties that elevate them above the brutes. Moral laws should be deduced from the knowledge of being God's creatures: first, an "enlightened self-love" (Wollstonecraft, 2008 [1790]: 33) that nourishes the hope in immortality and the constant striving for one's own perfection; second, the recognition "that on the general happiness depends their own", which impels men to "*do unto others what they wish they should do unto them*" (Wollstonecraft, 2011 [1794]: 293), that is, to act according to a maxim that can have universal value. We can submit our action to a universal principle and act in accordance with duty only if we see and respect our own humanity in others, but this possibility is precluded to women. Like the Victor Frankenstein recounted by her daughter Mary Shelley, therefore, for Wollstonecraft masculine domination breeds monsters and stops progress because it constitutionalizes hierarchies that prevent the realization of men and women as moral beings, which is only possible in a relationship among equals.

---

9 Cf. Kant, 1997 [1785]: sect. III; on Kant and Wollstonecraft, see Hunt Botting, 2016: 70–115.

This explains why Wollstonecraft considers the cause of her sex as "the cause of virtue", which moves her pen in her desire "to see woman placed in a station in which she would advance, instead of retarding, the progress of those glorious principles that give a substance to morality" (Wollstonecraft, 2014 [1792]: 21). Woman's cause is a universal cause: so long as she is incapable of recognizing her own humanity, because the masculine constitution of society obliges her to regard her own artificial dependence as a natural fact, every relationship of reciprocity with men will be impossible and the entire progress of the human race will be slowed, if not prevented.

Raising women from the dust and elevating them to the status of sovereign individuals is thus the goal of Wollstonecraft's emancipationist proposal. In order to achieve this, it is necessary in the first place that women, married or unmarried, have a "civil existence" in the state. Abolishing coverture and granting them a legal personality regardless of marriage is the condition for rendering "their private virtue a public benefit" (Wollstonecraft, 2014 [1792]: 178), since there can be no virtue where there is compulsion, and thus where marriage is a forced choice. For the same reason, women must be able to earn their livelihood and achieve what for Wollstonecraft is independence in the truest sense of the term: only industry, in fact, allows individuals to exercise their talents, so that material autonomy is also the prerequisite of moral autonomy (Wollstonecraft, 2014 [1792]: 113). Women, again, must receive a public education equal to that of men, in order to fully cultivate their intellect; they must, finally, have the right to vote, in order to take part in the formation of the will of the community of which they are part (Wollstonecraft, 2014 [1792]: 189, 176). For Wollstonecraft, as for Kant, law is the necessary mediation between the empirical individual and his moral freedom. It has the task of erasing, from a civil and political point of view, the asymmetries of power and relationships of dependence generated by masculine domination and the social dynamics to which it gives shape. In short, law must transform women into individuals so that society as a whole can be indefinitely perfected.

Like Rousseau, Wollstonecraft believes that the refinement of customs is a process of degeneration that has substituted the cult of appearance for the ancient practice of virtue, but she despises what she considers his nostalgia for the past and does not intend to renounce the benefits of civilization merely because she recognizes its defects (Rousseau, 1992 [1750]; Wollstonecraft 2008 [1790]: 39–40). Nature, for her, is not a state to return to, but a potential that should be developed in order to lay the foundations for indefinite moral progress. This potential, however, can only be translated into action within relationships with others, and it is precisely by criticizing the historical form of these relationships that Wollstonecraft illuminates their ordinary functioning and the 'naturally social' dynamics of the reproduction of masculine domination. These dynamics should be corrected by law, which, however, in turn expresses the degree of moral development achieved in a given stage of civilization. Thus, juridical mediation, which is the solution Wollstonecraft adopts in order to reconcile the abstract and the social (and therefore the sexed) individual, is not decisive. Sex can never be expelled from the social coordinates that constrain moral action or make it possible. It is the point of convergence between nature and society, it cannot be reduced to a purely physical datum, morally and legally indifferent, because it is always socially signified and organized within relations of domination (Wollstonecraft, 2014 [1792]: 23–24). This is evident in Wollstonecraft's own conclusions that once women have been granted their rights, the "common law of gravity prevailing, the sexes will fall into their proper places" (Wollstonecraft, 2014 [1792]: 24). The Newtonian lexicon – the overlap between customary and physical laws, between society and nature – expresses precisely the compelling efficacy of the masculine constitution of society and its ordinary dynamics of production and reproduction.[10]

Even when they have obtained their rights, therefore, women will continue to be defined in relation to men, to whom they are "connected ... as daughters, wives and mothers". However, they will perform their functions not by force but by choice, finally practicing a "conscious virtue" (Wollstonecraft, 2014 [1792]: 52). Thanks to emancipation, they will no longer have to mortify their intellectual capacities, but will be able to exercise them in the enclosure defined by the sexual division of labor with the knowledge appropriate to their reproductive role, and through the study of political science they will become "active citizens", educating their children to citizenship (Wollstonecraft, 2014 [1792]: 199, 175–177). The outcome of the emancipation invoked by Wollstonecraft thus ends up being a reconciliation between equality and subordination possible only through the miracle of "free obligation", which brings her closer not only to Kant, but also to her antagonist Rousseau.[11]

The republican perspective that animates her conclusions and leads to the re-signification of motherhood as a civic function[12] does not solve the problem of the masculine constitution of society, which continues to emerge not only as a remnant of the feudal past, but as a dominant character of modern politics. Wollstonecraft defines the "spirit of independence" that sustains the practice of virtue as "masculine" (Wollstonecraft, 2008 [1790]: 15). The same

---

10   On the transformations of the semantics of society between the eighteenth and nineteenth centuries, see Ricciardi, 2010: ch. 1.

11   On the paradox of "free obligation" see Riley, 1982.

12   For a republican interpretation of Wollstonecraft's work, see Halldenius, 2015.

term is used to describe the education that enabled women such as Sappho, Heloise, Catherine Macaulay, Catherine of Russia, and Madame d'Éon to act rationally and demonstrate that they are participants in a moral nature that has no sex because it pertains to the soul and not the body (Wollstonecraft, 2014 [1792]: 104). Under existing conditions, the independence and education necessary for the exercise of virtue remain a sexual privilege that the emancipation of women should remedy. Yet even as she envisions the order to come founded on equality, reciprocity, and cooperation between the sexes, Wollstonecraft calls it "manly" (Wollstonecraft, 2014 [1792]: 30).[13] The lexicon of virtue de-naturalizes behavior because it makes morality an accessible practice regardless of sex. Not even this practical conception of virtue, however, succeeds in ridding itself of the term's masculine roots and the sexed character that tradition and society have bestowed upon it, prescribing virtues to men and women which are differentiated by their sex. Both men and women are artificial beings. Both are to be considered individuals, therefore capable of moral action. In the end, however, it is the semantics of man that establishes the intrinsic character of the universal destination of humankind, and it is this masculine denotation of the universal that continues to univocally determine the concept of woman, making her the signifier of a position which is different because it is subordinate.

Even as she lays the groundwork for understanding and challenging the social conditions that establish this subordination, Wollstonecraft trusts in the emancipatory promise contained in the "simple principles" of the French Revolution. The woman in whose name she speaks therefore expresses the irreducible tension between a future not yet realized, in which she will finally be able to enjoy her rights, and the present that prevents her from exercising them. The singular woman who appears in the title of the *Vindication of the Rights of Woman* reflects this tension, because it expresses a universalistic ambition and at the same time identifies a socially determined position that is charged with accomplishing that ambition. Wollstonecraft, in fact, addresses the middle-class woman, who precisely by virtue of her position is already in the most favorable conditions for the deployment of her faculties. Although affected by the nefarious influence of aristocratic moral sentiments, that woman more than others is in a "natural state", in which the seeds of "false refinement" spread throughout society by the higher classes have taken root to a lesser extent (Wollstonecraft, 2014 [1792]: 30–31).[14] Polemically invoked

13   Cf. Gunther-Canada, 1996.
14   Cf. Wilcox, 2009. On the semantics of the middle class, see Battistini, 2022.

against the "partial civilization" that has hindered the proper exercise of human faculties by women, the nature that Wollstonecraft refers to is always and in any case an internal condition of society and the result of its dynamics, which position individuals not only according to sex, but also to property. The absence of privilege and the moderation of wealth make room for the active exercise of talents and thus the active practice of virtue. The 'natural woman' of the middle class thus announces an order in which small property and labor will make possible an overall discipline of social relations oriented towards an indefinite moral perfection, and in which education will be accessible to all without distinction, so that it is talents, and not ascribed privileges, that will distribute individuals in appropriate positions. Some men and women will be destined to become mechanical workers or servants, while others may aspire to govern or to support themselves, as Wollstonecraft herself did, through writing and the active exercise of their intellect (Wollstonecraft, 2014 [1792]: 31, 199).[15] In the order prefigured by her emancipationist proposal, therefore, the "furies of the hell" of the French Revolution, for whom work was not a vehicle of independence but a condition forced by poverty, are covered by the oblivion of the universal and are destined to find their place only in a subordinate position, without any possibility of fully enjoying the privilege of emancipation.

What Carole Pateman has called the "Wollstonecraft dilemma" should be reread in light of this contradiction. It is not only the quarrel between two opposing strategies of inclusion into citizenship, between the claim of emancipation that coincides with the achievement of equal and sexually "neutral" civil and political rights, and the legal recognition of specifically female functions and capacities (Pateman, 2003 [1980]: 96–7). By analyzing and criticizing the social process that produces woman as different, Wollstonecraft reclaims an equality that is always ultimately denied to women not only by masculine domination, but also by poverty. On the other hand, it is precisely the constant action of masculine domination that prevents us from considering the social constitution and its institutions, starting with citizenship, as a neutral space. When Wollstonecraft makes woman the absent subject of modern politics with the perspective of realizing its emancipatory promise, her universalistic ambition becomes, even beyond her intentions, the partial perspective that allows for the illumination of the fracture that divides the society of men, the line of conflict that with her and after her feminism would have practiced and deepened. The "Wollstonecraft dilemma" inaugurates modern feminism by confronting it

---

15   On Wollstonecraft's critique of the aristocratic distribution of property, cf. Ferguson, 1999 and Sapiro, 1992: 89 ff.

with the irreducible social determination of sexual experience, which others after her would confront in order to think about women's freedom in the face of the violence of slavery, racism, and capitalist industry.

2   The Matrix of Domination

In July 1837, the General Association of Congregational Churches of Massachusetts warns congregants of the dangers to "female character" from those women acting in public and speaking about "things which ought not to be named". Against this unacceptable novelty of the times, the letter's drafters invoke the New Testament to affirm that a woman should be "unobtrusive and private". Her quest for independence is a dishonor and a disgrace, since it was God who made her "dependent" in order to place her under the protection of man and enable her, within the appropriate sphere of life – namely, private life – to exercise her moral ascendancy over individuals and the nation. A woman may strive to spread Christian religion, piety, and benevolence, but she cannot take "the place and tone of man as a public reformer" without men putting themselves in "self-defence against her", without her character becoming "unnatural", without exposing society to degeneration and ruin (General Association of Massachusetts, 2000 [1837]: 119–121).

The women mentioned in this *Pastoral Letter* are the militants of the American Anti-Slavery Society, founded in 1833 by the journalist William Lloyd Garrison with the support of the Hicksite Quaker minister Lucretia Mott. The establishment of this association had intensified women's public presence, accelerating a process that had begun in the 1820s with the Moral Reform movement and had gone beyond the boundaries of the licit dissemination of Christian sentiments when women had begun to discuss "things which ought not to be named" such as male lust.[16] By the 1830s, abolitionists accentuate this encroachment, publicly denouncing the rapes of black slaves by their white masters as the most violent expression of that "passion". Adding guilt to guilt, they had invaded the political sphere with a campaign of anti-slavery petitions whose magnitude led Congress, in 1836, to pass a "gag rule" to prevent them from being followed up. The *Pastoral Letter* is only one example of the attitude of Protestant clergy, who saw their ecclesiastical authority threatened by the moral authority of militant women and their autonomous initiative for

---

16   Cf. Sklar, 2000: 8, 32; Walters, 1973.

salvation, encouraged by Garrison's religious radicalism.[17] It is also a symptom of the broader hostility toward the public speaking out of women who, through the reform and abolitionist movement, had established their political presence well before the suffragist movement appeared in Seneca Falls in 1848 and won the right to vote in 1920.[18] However, the *Pastoral Letter* is also particularly relevant because it elicits an immediate response from Sarah Grimké, who was on an abolitionist propaganda tour of New England with her sister Angelina in the summer of 1837. For the first time, two women were officially speaking in public as representatives of the Anti-Slavery Society, in front of an audience that was promiscuous in terms of race and gender. Moreover, these were white Southern women who, before fighting them, had been direct witnesses as masters to the horrors of slavery.[19] Responsible for such an important office, Sarah felt an obligation to respond to the pastors with one of her *Letters on the Equality of Sexes and the Condition of Woman*. In her view, by insisting on the moral influence that women would be empowered to exercise only on the condition of remaining "dependent", the *Pastoral Letter* expresses

> the flattering language of man since he laid aside the whip as a mean to keep woman in subjection. He spares her body; but the war he has waged against her mind, her heart, and her soul, has been no less destructive to her as a moral being. How monstrous, how anti-Christian is the doctrine that woman is dependent on man!
>
> GRIMKÉ, 2014 [1837a]: 40

With these words, Grimké explicitly calls out the social process of the production of women and their subordination, which for her, as for Wollstonecraft, generates monsters. The *Pastoral Letter* is thus reduced to a simple episode in the larger war of men against women, which Grimké takes upon herself to fight by becoming the protagonist of the battle for the immediate emancipation of slaves. Her challenge to masculine domination acquires meaning within this war and shows a fully political and social significance precisely through the discourse and practice that link the emancipation of slaves and that of women. Such discourse and such practice are symptoms of the transformation

---

17   Cf. DuBois, 1998: 55 ff; Lerner, 1979: 112–128. On the relationship between the Anti-Slavery Society and the black abolitionist movement, see Laudani, 2007: XIV ff.
18   Cf. Baritono, 2001.
19   For a biography of the Grimké sisters see Lerner, 1971; for an account of the originality of Sarah's arguments in support of women's rights also in comparison with her sister Angelina's, see Lerner, 1998.

sweeping the United States in the twenty years leading up to the Civil War, when the market revolution redefined the social conditions of American freedom, and the Second Great Religious Awakening allowed those who could not enjoy it to express their dissatisfaction.[20] Struggling against masculine domination, Grimké discovers an oppression that crosses all epochs while being historical, that defines the internal organization of social space and the way in which sex marks a different experience of time, and that determines the intensity of exploitation and the specific valorization and devaluation of the free and slave labor force. In her reflection, the concept of woman expresses the tension between an irrepressible partiality and the ambition to achieve universal liberation in her name.

Even though she starts from the reading of the sacred texts and is in continuity with Astell (whom she had never read) and the "biblical feminism" that animated the America of the Second Great Awakening, Grimké develops a critique of masculine domination that takes place on a historical and symbolic, and therefore social, level. In her *Letters*, in fact, she observes that, for man, woman is a "property" (Grimké, 2014 [1837a]: 38) from which he can profit, making her an instrument at the service of his own pleasure. To the question "what is a woman?", man has answered "she is female". He has exalted "the animal above the intellectual" (Grimké, 2014 [1837a]: 63) and thus justified the outrageous subjugation of creatures that God made equally intelligent and responsible. In this way, "in all ages and countries, not even excepting enlightened republican America", she has been reduced to a means of man's welfare. This reduction to object and means requires Grimké to place women and slaves side by side "in oppression", as both make the male "lust" for domination that operates in American plantation society clear (Grimké, 2014 [1837a]: 37). Their association is not metaphorical, insofar as for Grimké the difference between the whip that strikes bodies and the discipline that "crushes" minds cannot be erased (Grimké 2014 [1837b]: 27 and 2014 [1837a]: 41).[21] On the contrary, precisely by reversing the use of slavery as a metaphor for the absence of freedom common to the political debate of her time,[22] Grimké makes the subordination of woman the first historical example and thus the symbol of all oppression. She is the "first victim" of the "unhallowed passion" of men (Grimké, 2014 [1837a]: 36). Her subjugation has become traditional and ordinary being at least in part deprived of the coercion which has instituted it. Precisely because of this, the woman's standpoint allows us to bring to light

---

20   Cf. Foner, 1998: ch. 5 and 6; Stokes and Conway, 1996.
21   Cf. Casadei, 2016: 5–15.
22   Cf. Foner, 1998: 50.

the fully societal character achieved by masculine domination. The latter literally gives shape to American society, organizes its space and institutions, and becomes the legitimizing foundation of all the hierarchies – not just the sexed ones – that traverse it.[23]

The conception of women as objects of property is the expression of the way in which American society produces and reproduces itself by assigning specific positions in the sexual division of labor to men and women through the systematic distinction between the "appropriate spheres" for the two sexes. It is a distinction constantly present in the American political discourse of the first half of the nineteenth century, when the market revolution invested the domestic space, transforming it from an autonomous productive unit into a privileged place for women's labor, necessary for the reproduction of agricultural and waged-labor, for women's work in the home to support the nascent manufacturing industry and, lastly, for the privacy that allows the American citizen to intimately enjoy his freedom.[24] According to Grimké, through the identification of woman and female and the consequent distinction between "masculine and feminine" virtues, the man procures "an house-keeper, whose chief business is in the kitchen, or the nursery", but also to please him sexually (Grimkè, 2014 [1837a]: 40, 44). Thus, the woman is "trained" to think of herself up to her concept, as "a kind of machinery, necessary to keep the domestic engine in order, but of little value as the intelligent companion of men" (Grimké, 2014 [1837a]: 63). Educated from childhood to consider herself an inferior creature, woman does not have "that self-respect which conscious equality would engender" (Grimké, 2014 [1837a]: 65) and for this reason, when her virtue is assailed, she easily yields to the flattery of man, in the belief that the relationship with a being considered superior can raise her too. In this way, a "false and debasing estimate" pushes the woman to take part in her own submission, defines the private as her "appropriate sphere", and leads her to devote herself to the superficial cult of fashion in order to attract the attention of men, as well as to consider marriage as "the only thing needful" (Grimké, 2014 [1837a]: 62).

It is precisely in marriage that the fully social character of masculine domination is manifested, as well as the symbolic and institutional connection between the oppression of women and that of slaves. In particular, the institution of coverture establishes on the legal level what the reduction of the woman to a simple object of property affirms on the symbolic one, since the

---

23   On the semantic shift between "social" and "societal", see Ricciardi, 2010: 48; on the societal character of masculine domination, see Bourdieu, 2001 [1998].

24   Cf. Foner, 1998: 57.

"very being" of a wife is absorbed in the person of the husband, just as that of slaves is in their master (Grimké, 2014 [1837a]: 81). A husband can squander a wife's entire dowry, and she – like slaves – will have no chance to assert herself against him in court, because she is considered by law to be part of his person (Grimké, 2014 [1837a]: 82). For the same reason, a married woman cannot acquire any property, so that the fruits of her labor will end up entirely in her husband's pockets (Grimké, 2014 [1837a]: 84). While she considers the law as an expression of a dominion that is affirmed and reproduced even with "brute force, the law of violence", Grimké contrasts marriage as a "divine ordination" with marriage as a "civil contract", because in the former she believes that the mutual moral perfection of creatures made equal by God can be realized (Grimké, 2014 [1837a]: 91, 88). The principle of equality between the sexes, justified theologically, allows her to denounce the fundamental inequality that survives within the "contract", even when its stipulation presupposes formal equality between the parties. Her critique thus retraces the same arguments proposed by Astell and Wollstonecraft, and this is inevitable, because patriarchal ideology manifests elements of profound continuity that from the early modern age reach the global one, characterizing itself as the timeless core of political and social discourse. However, its effects change according to the different regimes of historicity in which it operates, and it is this change that must be detected in the years leading up to the American Civil War, when slavery and the oppression of women create the conditions for the establishment of free wage labor and manufacture.

Grimké's emphasis on the problem of property ownership and wages in fact shifts the gaze to the way in which masculine domination determines women's differential entry into the American labor market as free commodities. The "general opinion that women are inferior to men" has "tremendous effects on the laboring classes" because it places a "disproportionate value" on women's time and labor (Grimké, 2014 [1837a]: 64). Whether in occupations considered specifically feminine – such as sewing and laundry, commonly done in the home – or in wage labor at home for manufacturing, or again in occupations such as teaching, women's wages are systematically lower than men's (Grimké, 2014 [1837a]: 65). This devaluation of women's work corresponds to their sexual valorization, which prompts many female workers to spend part of their wages on clothes, "to be as well attired as her employer" (Grimké, 2014 [1837a]: 79). In the society of her time, Grimké sees the "man's social symbolic labor" at work (Irigaray, 1987 [1974]: 135), the process of patriarchal signification or valorization of women's bodies that not only effectively forces them into the roles prescribed by the sexual division of labor, but also causes them to enter the market in a subordinate position.

Thus, while the debate over slavery that inflamed Jacksonian America was articulated through the opposition between free and slave labor, Grimké shows their continuity, which consists not so much or only in the lack of autonomy understood as possession of one's person or economic independence, but in the way masculine domination determines specific modes of valorization and exploitation. As the buying and selling of slaves in Asia and Africa demonstrates, women are not only reduced to "saleable commodities", but their value is "set upon personal charms, just as a handsome horse commands a high price" (Grimké, 2014 [1837a]: 47–49). Similarly, women were valued sexually as domestic machines and instruments of pleasure in the marriage market established by British colonizers in the Indian colonies to make up for the shortage of wives. While proponents of free labor claim as a measure of freedom a "mans wage" that allows men to support their families without their wives being forced in turn to work,[25] Grimké shows that the family is one of the main institutions through which masculine domination operates, establishing the specific mode of exploitation of labor within and outside the home, and that sex is the operator that continually determines the valorization and devaluation of women's labor, free and slave, in the marketplace.

The comparison between the different conditions of women in history and in the world – which she develops using the work of the abolitionist feminist Lidia Mary Child[26] – allows Grimké to demonstrate that, insofar as it is the matrix of every relationship of super- and subordination, masculine domination has a doubly historical character. It is a historical constant, because its action is evident in every place and in all epochs. At the same time, it takes on a specific configuration depending on the place, the epoch, and the social position of its subjects. This constant variation in continuity is manifested in the varying intensity of violence, ranging from the physical coercion of the whip to the subtler coercion of "toys and trifles" (Grimké, 2014 [1837a]: 55) that lead women to adhere to the set of behaviors that masculine domination demands of them. It depends on the different conditions of production, which explain why – in less evolved societies – women's labor has been socially valued much more than in the present time (Grimké, 2014 [1837a]: 58). The intensity of violence that oppresses women changes with their social position, since the refinement of customs protects, at least in part, women of the higher classes from the domestic brutality of their husbands and from rape, to which women of the working classes and black slaves are more exposed (Grimké, 2014

---

25   Cf. Foner, 1998: 74 ff; Lerner, 1971: 15–30.
26   Cf. Child, 1835.

[1837a]: 89).[27] In Grimke's discourse, the concept of woman does not define a homogeneous condition but is grasped in all its historical depth. The centrality of history, however, does not exclude the possibility of considering the oppression of women as the matrix and symbol of all oppression, thus making it the perspective point to radicalize the judgment on the present society through the association with slavery:

> Here I am reminded of the resemblance between the situation of women in heathen and Mohammedan countries, and our brethren and sisters of color in the Christian land, where they are despised and cast out as though they were unclean. And on precisely the same ground, because they are said to be inferior. The treatment of women as wives is almost uniformly the same in all heathen countries.
>
> GRIMKÉ, 2014 [1837a]: 53

Thanks to the similarity with the condition of slaves in the United States, the contrast between pagan and Christian women fades away, to the point of questioning the progressive conception of history that from 1845 would be expressed with the formula of "manifest destiny". Grimké's feminist critique shows that it is not possible to codify history, identified with the "traditions of men" (Grimké, 2014 [1837a]: 38), according to an advance/delay scheme:[28] it can be progressive for men only as long as it keeps women in a condition of subordination considered natural and therefore immutable. By making the concept of woman the general signifier of oppression, Grimké recognizes in masculine domination the principle that unites and synchronizes conditions as distant as they are heterogeneous. It exerts itself on difference and on differences, aiming at subjecting them to its logic, and therefore at homologating them, by force or by the habit consolidated in tradition.

According to Grimké, the coercion exerted by masculine domination permeates the entire society and for this very reason does not coincide with the use of force alone, just as it does not end with the obligation imposed by law, but acts on minds and in thought. Masculine domination produces its subjects, that is, it simultaneously gives shape to those who dominate and those who are dominated, and in this way, it becomes a "system" (Grimké, 2014 [1837a]: 27). However, although they are its product, the subjects of masculine domination are not equal or even equivalent to each other. On the one hand, "the lust of

---

27   In the unpublished fragment titled *Marriage,* from 1855, Grimké denounces sexual violence as an ordinary practice in marriage. Cf. Grimké, 1988 [1855].

28   Cf. Koselleck, 2004 [1979]: 222 ff.

dominion inevitably produces hardness of heart" (Grimké, 2014 [1837a]: 27)
and those who possess unlimited power also cultivate the desire to exercise it.
On the other hand, laws that deprive women of all power, freedom and responsibility, "have a tendency to lessen them in their own estimation as moral and
responsible beings" and lead them to seek "protection and indulgence" from
their oppressor (Grimké, 2014 [1837a]: 87). Masters and slaves, men and women
are placed in asymmetrical and antithetical positions within social relations in
which sexual difference and the stigma of slavery overlap with that between
being owners and being owned.

What results from this system and ensures it over time is a 'hierarchical
thought' capable of binding the minds of each and every one as a "superstition" (Grimké, 2014 [1837a]: 38). This capacity explains how the force with
which man has asserted his dominance has been able to gain the continuity
over time necessary to establish a tradition, and how this tradition has been
consolidated to the point of being believed by those who experience it. The
laws of North Carolina, Grimké recalls, punish anyone who tries to teach slaves
to read and write, with the explicit argument that this "tends to excite dissatisfaction in their minds, and to produce insurrection and rebellion" (Grimké,
2014 [1837a]: 21). Under the same pretense of keeping her in awe, men ridicule
the woman if she tries to enter the "temple of science and literature" (Grimké,
2014 [1837a]: 75) because otherwise she would not stay at home to attend to her
duties as a wife and a mother. Slaves and women must be kept in ignorance of
their own possibilities in order to accept their subjugation and the productive
functions society assigns to them while the man benefits. By insisting on wom-
en's animal faculties and erasing their intellectual faculties, masculine domination produces the matrix of a social order built on slavery and property,
the sexual division of labor, and the division between manual and intellectual
labor, which for Grimké overlap. By placing minds in "shackles" it acts so that
no one can ever "forget the distinction between male and female" and so that
everyone accepts the inevitability of domination (Grimké, 2014 [1837a]: 111, 44).

Precisely because Grimké recognizes that masculine domination produces
not only women, but society as a whole, her claim to equality of the sexes before
God is charged with a specific political valence and design against the existing
order. The only way for women to achieve their equality is to take direct part in
the struggle for the immediate emancipation of slaves:

One of the most striking characteristics of modern times is the tendency
toward a universal dissemination of knowledge in all Protestant commu-
nities. But the character of woman has been elevated more by partici-
pating in the great moral enterprises of the day, than by anything else. It

would astonish us if we could see at a glance all the labor, the patience, the industry, the fortitude which woman has exhibited, in carrying on the causes of Moral Reform, Anti-Slavery &c.

GRIMKÉ, 2014 [1837a]: 77–78

Masculine domination has never completely erased the "incessant struggle [of women] to rise to that degree of dignity, which God designed [them] to possess" (Grimké, 2014 [1837a]: 119), but the abolitionist cause intensifies and accelerates it because it challenges the most violent social manifestation of oppression. The abolitionist cause is the cause of women's emancipation because it allows them to "forget their sex", to stop identifying with their oppression and to finally "feel equal" (Grimké, 2014 [1837a]: 45, 111). Equality is not so much the presupposition as the result of women's political action to interrupt the social production of difference as subordination. By devoting themselves to activities in accordance with their intellectual and moral capacities, they will reduce the time allocated to housework, practically calling into question the distinction between "masculine and feminine virtues" and the corresponding distinction between the "appropriate spheres" of the two sexes. A husband – who, after all, cannot expect a table set for him every day – will then have to make do with bread, butter, and potatoes (Grimké, 2014 [1837a]: 63), with good peace even for those abolitionists who, like Catharine Beecher, believed that women should accept their "subordinate situation" to men and be content to exercise their moral influence in private (Beecher, 1835).

The contestation of the separation between the spheres, however, involves the politicization of the domestic sphere, with the aim of removing the functions of wife and mother from the private use that men have historically done to satisfy their own interest. The positions of wife and mother for Grimké are not a destiny – in fact, she admits that a woman may not marry, as she did (Grimké, 2014 [1837a]: 85) – nor are they valued for their civic function, as they were for Wollstonecraft and the American tradition of "republican motherhood". Rather, they constitute the starting point for disrupting masculine domination by freeing minds from the superstition that shackles them. This task is all the more relevant because women have historically been agents of the reproduction of masculine domination. Indeed, a mother who considers herself nothing more than an instrument of pleasure teaches her daughter to coquet, in the hope of acquiring at least "a precarious ascendancy over her absolute master" (Grimké, 2014 [1837a]: 53). A woman elevated to her proper position, on the other hand, will be able to teach her children to consider themselves, like her, moral and responsible beings, and thus to lose "the animal nature of man and woman" (Grimké, 2014 [1837a]: 46). The "domestic duties", therefore, are not denied by the affirmation of the equality between the sexes – which also has a precise tactical reason, since denying them would have aroused general public condemnation of politically engaged women – but the roles of mother and wife are re-signified in a project of "moral reformation" openly oriented to challenge the conditions of the reproduction of masculine domination (Grimké, 2014 [1837a]: 55–56).

By questioning the separation between public and private, political and domestic, Grimké thus gives the claim to rights a meaning that is not reducible to the recognition of women's civil and political personhood invoked by Wollstonecraft and emancipationist feminism after her. The goal of women's and slaves' emancipation is of course central, and in Grimké's perspective – which also differs from a part of the abolitionist movement that is reluctant to openly claim women's rights – the two causes are inseparable.[29] However, Grimké's feminism draws its strength from a mobilization of women that was not even imaginable in late eighteenth-century Europe and that, precisely through the struggle for women's emancipation and the abolition of slavery, in the United States had brought to light the fully societal character of masculine domination. When she speaks of "human rights" (Grimké, 2014 [1837a]: 61), therefore, Grimké is not only referring to the inalienable attributes of every creature of God that law should recognize and sanction, but to the act of rejecting oppression and thus "arising" to the height of one's moral stature, "in the majesty of femininity" (Grimké, 2014 [1837a]: 91), which significantly takes the place of the "humanity" of the rights being claimed, and which is not configured as a pre-social attribute, but as a force to be conquered in the struggle against existing social conditions.

The acknowledged centrality of action allows us to decipher the greeting that concludes each of the *Letters on the Equality of Sexes*. Addressing her interlocutor Mary S. Parker, president of the Boston Female Anti-Slavery Society, Grimké writes: "thine for the oppressed in the bonds of womanhood" (Grimké, 2014 [1837a]: 35). Womanhood consists in recognizing each other not only 'as' the oppressed, but 'on the side' of the oppressed, making the rejection of oppression a shared project of transformation. It is invoked to constitute women as a collective subject through abolitionist militancy, it breaks the individualism of the discourse of rights – which forty years later Elizabeth Cady Stanton would define as the "solitude of the self" that founds the autonomy of women as individuals (Cady Stanton, 1981 [1882]) – and explains the pressing political rhetoric of the *Letters*: how can a woman devote herself to her home,

---

29   Cf. Lerner, 1998: 19–20 and Sklar, 2000: 25–26.

her husband and her children, and seek in privacy her "selfish enjoyments" for-getting "her brethren and sisters in bondage"? (Grimké, 2014 [1837a]: 57) How can an American woman consider herself morally "pure" when she sees her slave sisters seduced and violated, knowing that her husband is responsible for this violence? Can she say "I have nothing to do with slavery? She cannot and be guiltless" (Grimké, 2014 [1837a]: 67). By pointing to the possibility of a bond between the oppressed against oppression, Grimké alters the language of rights because she brings to light the material and symbolic violence that sus-tains the freedom of the American people. Her invocation shows the existence of a part that, by refusing to be dominated, promises an emancipation finally untethered from the existence of hierarchies and their reproduction, and in this way activates a polarization and fracture within the modern political universal. When it reaches the height of its "majesty", the concept of woman becomes more than just the general signifier of oppression and is charged, by virtue of its partiality, with a universal promise of liberation.

3 The Black Word

In 1851 at the Women's Convention in Akron, Ohio, a man uses the association between women and slaves to deny the rights of both because of their shared lack of intellect. What women can expect, given the obvious weakness of their sex, is to be helped into carriages and over puddles. Responding to these argu-ments, the militant abolitionist and black suffragist Sojourner Truth, who was born a slave, asks the audience the question "Ain't I a woman?" The question echoes through the room four times, pressing: "I have ploughed and planted, and gathered into barns, and no man could head me! And ain't I a woman? I could work as much and eat as much as a man ... I have borne thirteen chil-dren, and see most all sold off to slavery ... And ain't I a woman?" (Truth, 1992 [1851]: 491). Christ, after all – Sojourner Truth says –, was born without the contribution of a man. He was the son of a woman and God, which suggests how much power women can gain when they act together, claiming for them-selves and the slaves the rights to which they are entitled.[30] With the impetus of a Shakespearean Shylock, Truth gives voice to the difference that slavery imprints on sexed experience, highlighting an antagonism that was not artic-ulated in Grimké's association between women and slaves. In the plantation

---

30   For a review of the use of Truth's discourse in feminist political theory, see Haraway, 1992: 99, n. 10.

system, the positions of the lady and the slave are represented as distinct and opposing figures to be dominated in an economy of exploitation that valorizes sexual difference in the domestic and productive spheres, making the master's despotism over the black woman the condition of possibility for the privileged subjection of the white woman. Speaking as a woman against the racist interdiction imposed by masculine domination, Truth challenges the plantation society.

Fifty years later, slavery has been abolished, but the "color line" (Douglass, 1992 [1883]: 92–96) continues to cut through American society, marking the experience of millions of women and men. After Reconstruction, the nascent social sciences ensured the resilience of the discourse of rights by justifying the subordination of blacks on the basis of their presumed natural inferiority. The Spencerian lexicon of the struggle for survival puts biological determinism in the service of racism and reinforces masculine domination and the rigid Victorian morality that asserts itself in the second half of the century, supporting the transition to industrial capitalism. The Lady becomes the socially recognized representation of what women should be – a femininity fully identified with the duties of wives and mothers, functional to the evolution of the species and the progress of civilization. While racism is configured as the social science of a practice of oppression, even those who challenge it are forced to make the language of evolutionism their own, which sits alongside, overlaps or replaces the theological-political.[31] The scientific appeal to nature is all the more necessary when those whom it should condemn to subordination or extinction do not meekly accept it. In 1848 the Seneca Falls Convention marks a step forward in the collective organization of women in favor of the full attainment of civil and political rights and triggers, even for this, a tension between the "woman question" and the "Negro problem".[32] The autonomous organization of black people, on the other hand, becomes more and more intense, giving rise to practices of solidarity in which women are the protagonists. Anna Julia Cooper – who was born a slave in 1858 and died at the age of 106 after earning a PhD at the Sorbonne, and always in the forefront of the battle for the classical education of blacks that she herself had given to hundreds of students, women and men[33] – speaks out in the crucial historical transition of the end of the century. With the slave plantation behind her and the factory

31   Cf. Alridge, 2007: 416–446; Degler, 1991: ch. 5 and Hawkins, 1997: ch. 2.
32   Cf. Baritono, 2001: LXIV ff; Lerner, 1979: 99–105.
33   On Cooper's life see Johnson, 2008. Cooper's PhD dissertation was entitled *L'Attitude de la France a l'égard de l'esclavage Pendant la Revolution*. An analysis of the work is provided by May, 2007: ch. IV.

on the horizon, her critique of racist and patriarchal society led her to claim a leading role for the Black Woman in the social order that has reduced her to silence. In this way, while Cooper accepts the evolutionary laws of that order, she shows that racism and masculine domination are constitutional factors of American society in transition to industrial capitalism.

> In the clash and clatter of our American Conflict, it has been said that the South remains Silent. Like the Sphinx she inspires vociferous disputation, but herself takes little part in the noisy controversy. One muffled strain in the silent South, a jarring chord and a vague and uncomprehended cadenza has been and still is the Negro. And of that muffled chord, the one mute and voiceless note has been the sadly expectant Black Woman, *An infant crying in the night // An infant crying for the light // And with no language – but a cry.*
>
> COOPER, 1998 [1892]: 51

By signing *A Voice from the South* (1892)[34] as "a black woman from the South", Cooper makes a silence speak: not a lament but the yearning to come out of the darkness, the tension towards the articulation of a sound muffled by the din of many voices, the mute note of a symphony that disappears into the whole, which in isolation refers to an incomprehensible un-tuned sound, but one that still rings out and must be heard. The Black Woman comes after "the Negro". He is the "*cul de sac* of the nation", the "ghost" that haunts the American conscience, that provokes endless harangues and yet remains, in this hubbub, the "dumb skeleton in the closet", hidden and never consulted by the many "Caucasian barristers" who analyze and dissect, theorize and synthesize, but never put themselves in his shoes and at best make a ridiculous caricature (Cooper, 1998 [1892]: 51–52, 139). Yet, neither could the "Negro" fully and adequately reproduce the voice of the Black Woman, nor can the white woman who "would like to help 'elevate' the colored people (in her own way of course and so long as they understand their place)" (Cooper, 1998 [1892]: 88). Like the "subaltern woman" whose silence Gayatri Chakravorty Spivak gives voice to in thinking about the reproductive dynamics of the global order of capital, Cooper's Black Woman is unrepresentable because she occupies a "unique position" in the society of her time: in "a period of itself transitional and unsettled", she simultaneously confronts the "women's question" and the "race

---

34   The essays collected in *A Voice from the South* (Cooper, 1998) were written between 1886 and 1891.

problem", and is an "unknown or unacknowledged" factor for both of them. Of all the forces that move civilization, she is the "least ascertainable and definitive" (Cooper, 1998 [1892]: 112). From this uncertain and promising position speaks Anna Julia Cooper, who need not put herself in the Black Woman's shoes because she herself is a Black woman.[35]

Confronted by the signs in the waiting room of a Southern train station – "For Ladies" and "For Colored People" – Cooper has the experience of being out of place, and asks herself, "which head I come?" (Cooper, 1998 [1892]: 95) The question does not signal a "double consciousness", as W.E.B. Du Bois defined the condition that leads Black people to look at themselves through the eyes of others and to split their gaze on reality (Du Bois, 1897). The Black Woman does not even embody two distinguishable positions that are contingently intertwined, because the adjective re-signifies the noun, because the color line radically redetermines the sexed experience. Insofar as she is placeless, her position is unique: not just one among many witnesses to be heard in the great trial of the American nation, but the one who – while silent – was "open-eyed" and saw, becoming the accurate "calorimeter" of every "social atmospheric condition" (Cooper, 1998 [1892]: 51–52). Since she is black, the woman who speaks out offers the partial perspective from which to observe how the historical constant of masculine domination is transformed when racism becomes a stable social operator, and thus to judge the state of American civilization from within its movement.

The transformation of the "race problem" is already an index of this movement, marked by the shift from slavery to "colorphobia" (Cooper, 1998 [1902]: 208), two conditions that Cooper ties together by using categories borrowed from evolutionary social science and biological theories of heredity against their racist effects. Emancipation has defeated any attempt – such as the one pursued by phrenology – to justify the subordination of blacks on the basis of their physical nature, so it is a matter of offering a scientifically social understanding of that subordination. Blacks are a product of the condition in which they have been held. Against what the theories of atavism assert, no individual character can be separated from previous generations and the circumstances of its growth (Cooper, 1998 [1892]: 164). Consequently,

> our present poverty is due to the fact that the toil of the last quarter century enriched these coffers, but left us the heirs of crippled, deformed,

---

35   Cf. Alexander, 1995.

frost-bitten, horny-handed and empty-handed mothers and fathers. Oh,
the shame of it!

COOPER, 1998 [1892]: 143

Racism is the legacy of slavery branded on the skin of millions of men and
women. This is why the black man cannot be the "arbiter of his own destiny"
(Cooper, 1998 [1892]: 61–62) and, as a worker, suffers "cut throat competition"
(Cooper, 1998 [1902]: 208). Racism generates poor labor and so slavery continues to operate within the free labor market, putting blacks at a disadvantage in
what Cooper, using Herbert Spencer's vocabulary, calls a "struggle for survival".

   Woman, like the "Negro", is also a product of history. Christianity and feudal
customs have contributed to the construction of the modern ideal: the former has sown the seed to consider her beyond all ranks, according to the same
moral code of man. The latter made her an object of reverence and protection thanks to chivalry. Yet, the seed sown by Christianity germinated without
blooming, and in the Middle Ages as in the modern era men only have "respect
for the elect few among whom they expect consort" (Cooper, 1998 [1892]: 55).
Woman thus found herself with no God-designated destiny for herself, no aspirations, or work of her own, or duty to herself beyond that of pleasing man.
The "one-sided masculine definition" of what is "womanly" (Cooper, 1998
[1892]: 73) historically operates to limit her possibilities: the ban on access to
higher education – which in the United States began to be repealed at the state
level in 1833, when women were first allowed to enroll in a college – tried to
stop time on the threshold of the century, when Sylvain Maréchal proposed in
France his *Projet de loi portant défense d'apprendre à lire aux femmes* (Maréchal
1801). The transgressive action of feminists active in the Bluestocking Society
was the bogeyman to justify the education ban from the opposition between
the wife and the educated woman, regarding the latter as "unsex" and inclined
to remain a "spinster" as if "the intellectual woman [was] not desirable in the
matrimonial market". The one-sided definition of what a woman is then crys-
tallizes the society of "separate spheres", in which she is the "absolute queen
of the drawing room" (Cooper, 1998 [1892]: 80, 84, 91), within the concept. It is
no accident that for Cooper precisely educated women give "a deeper, richer,
nobler, and grander meaning to the word womanly" (Cooper, 1998 [1892]: 73).

   Masculine domination constantly reproduces the same ideological appara-
tus, but the Black Woman has an entirely specific experience of oppression. "A
Negro Woman cannot be a Lady", and therefore she is not entitled to the attention and care of men. On the contrary, it is possible to brutally attack her, throw
her out of train cars, push her out of her seat, or hit and injure her (Cooper,
1998 [1892]: 64, 93). Sojourner Truth's pressing question resonates silently in

Cooper's words, establishing a continuity between the violence of the present and the violence of the plantation: the same people who today despise and fear the mixing of races have forced black women to accept it through rape. While forcing her to irrigate the soil of the South with blood and tears, slavery deprived the Black Woman of everything: of her own person, making her a property at the disposal of a master's arbitrariness; of a home, of education, of money, of the habit of acquiring it through work (Cooper, 1998 [1893]: 202). The Black Woman, however, has always worked to the point of becoming, by the end of the century, the main source of income for her family. If she can be defined as a "domestic servant" (Cooper, 1998 [1902]: 208), therefore, it is not only as an "indoor partner" of the family business, taking care of the mundane and maternal duties by contributing to what the "outdoor manager who conducts the business and controls the wages" earns, but also for the work she does in the service of a mistress (Cooper, 1898: 295–298). Redetermined by slavery and then by racism, the concept of woman becomes the signifier of a sexed social despotism that routinely acts through violence, as well as a hierarchization of domestic space in which the color line and salary diversify women's positions within the same sexual division of labor.

The description of the Black Woman's experience is not meant to offer a more correct phenomenology of oppression or a complete classification of differences. Precisely because she is the silent part of the "race problem" and the "woman question", her perspective allows us to see how power also reproduces itself within oppression, determining lines of tension and antagonism that limit the possibilities for liberation. Thus, Black men are simultaneously agents of masculine domination and racism: they, too, believe that women should not have a higher education and can be content "worshipping masculinity" (Cooper, 1998 [1892]: 85) and gaining some advantage by compromising with the master and betraying their own race, driving their wives to leave their homes to protect themselves and their children. The common racist oppression does not erase the domination that each man claims to exercise over all women, nor does it define an identity of interests among those who suffer it in different sexed positions. For their part, white women – like the members of the *Wimodaugsis* Club, who have banned a black woman from membership – seem to believe that color does not allow her to be a wife, mother, daughter, or sister like them. The color that the Black Woman wears opens a "Pandora's box ... in the ideal harmony of this modern Eden without an Adam" (Cooper, 1998 [1892]: 88), clearly showing that women's position in society, as well as their oppression, is not homogeneous. For this reason, Cooper is not surprised that rather late in the day, and "after much courting", the national and international movement for the emancipation of women obtained "the gracious smile of

the Southern woman – I beg her pardon – the Southern lady" (Cooper, 1998
[1902]: 100). The apology signals the specific interest in remaining a mistress
that is expressed in the racism of the Southern white woman, who is convinced
that every black person is a slave because her grandfather owned black slaves.
Any generalization that erases difference reproduces the power that produces
oppression. There is no "woman question" that can be ended by getting men
out of the way, because racism determines the quality and intensity of sexual
oppression by placing some in the position of master or mistress and others
in the position of slave or domestic servant. All women are oppressed, but not
all women are equal in oppression. It is not possible to say that women are "all
of one mind" because that "all" is likely to "stick in the throat of the Southern
woman" (Cooper, 1998 [1892]: 97). The Black Woman's speaking out, therefore,
does not merely challenge masculine domination, but also assaults the racist
conditions of its reproduction, just as it comes to terms with the differences
that racist patriarchy has accrued among women.

The color line thus establishes a political difference: "the white woman could
at least plead for her own emancipation; the black woman, doubly enslaved,
could but suffer and struggle and be silent" (Cooper, 1998 [1893]: 202). However,
in silence the Black Woman has struggled, and that is precisely why her silence
must be heard:

> all through the darkest period of the colored women's oppression in this
> country her yet unwritten history is full of heroic struggle, a struggle
> against fearful and overwhelming odds, that often ended in a horrible
> death, to maintain and protect that which woman holds dearer in life.
> The painful, patient and silent toil of mothers to gain a fee simple title
> to the bodies of their daughters, the despairing fight as on an entrapped
> tigress, to keep hallowed their own persons, would furnish material for
> epics.[36]
>
> COOPER, 1998 [1902]: 202

The epics of the black woman to whom Cooper gives voice inaugurates her
ethics because she narrates oppression starting from the struggle against it and
transforms the latter into the universal "responsibility" (Cooper, 1998 [1892]:117)
of reactivating and pushing forward the movement of civilization by initiating
what black writer and activist Frances E.W. Harper has called "woman's era"

---

36   The epic battle of which Cooper speaks is the same that Sethe, the runaway slave protag-
     onist of Toni Morrison's masterpiece, fights going so far as to kill her daughter to prevent
     her from falling into the hands of the slave master (Morrison, 1987).

(Harper, 1893: 434). For Cooper, being a woman "is sublime" in the face of "the gateway of this new era of American civilization", because as a mother she is the first to form the man by "directing the earliest impulses of his character" (Cooper, 1998 [1892]: 117, 59). What is even greater is the privilege of the Black Woman, who has defended tooth and nail the "ideals of womanhood" (Cooper, 1998 [1893]: 202) and is now called upon to embody them in the fullest way, as a mother just as much as with her intellect, which through higher education can become a "dynamic factor" in society (Cooper, 1998 [1892]: 77).

"The memory of past oppression and the fact of present attempted repression" are likewise signs of an "irrepressible power" and give her the great responsibility of being the one who "can move the lever" that triggers the movement (Cooper, 1998 [1892]: 117, 62). The Black Woman becomes an evolutionary agent capable of introducing moral levees – God, Home, Native Land – to the utilitarianism that dominated in the era of accumulation, when man pursued his selfish desire for profit at the price of black rights and the interest of the homeland, thus generating internecine warfare (Cooper, 1998 [1892]: 111). To put it in terms borrowed from Spencer – whom Cooper despises for his agnosticism, but who uses bending the dominant language of the nascent social science to her own ends (Cooper, 1998 [1892]: 191) – the Black Woman is the one who can trigger the transition from a military society to an industrial society, in which cooperation prevails over the law of the strongest and the racism it has generated. The "survival of the fittest" (Cooper, 1998 [1913]: 219) is made possible by the capacity for adaptation that the Negro himself has shown in history through his submission (Cooper, 1998 [1892]: 144). In order for society to evolve, therefore, it is necessary to remove the obstacles that prevent Blacks, as well as women, from having access to the "struggle for bread" on fair terms (Cooper, 1898), so that in this humanity regenerated by racial equality, each person can simply try to improve himself or herself and his or her condition and mind his and her own business. Different individualities are the necessary components of an order that can be harmonious without renouncing conflict: only differences make possible the composition of diverse sounds in a single score. This conflictual harmony is what the Black Woman invokes against racism, opposing the shouting "America to Americans!", the deportations of Chinese or Italians, the expulsion of blacks through the colonization of Mexico or Africa, and lynchings, whose only effect would be to block the movement of civilization. All of these subjects, for Cooper, "are the Americans", and no group can be "supreme", for it is the differences that have lived in America since its origin – Native Americans, Pilgrims, and black Africans – that have made its republican form and democratic administration "necessary". Alexis de Tocqueville is therefore wrong to see the principle of the failure of the republic in the difference between the races. There is a history that has not yet been written: after Asia and Europe, now America is the last page marking "the final triumph of universal reciprocity born of universal conflict with forces that cannot be exterminated" (Cooper, 1892: 127–129).[37]

The hope of advancement toward this regenerated humanity rests, according to Cooper, first and foremost "on the homelife and on the influence of good women in those homes" (Cooper, 1998 [1892]: 55), and it is for this reason that her voice was listened to with distrust by a part of feminism, instead gaining centrality within the history of the black struggle for classical education – alongside W.E.B. Du Bois in his clash with B.T. Washington – and in the genealogy of African American political theory.[38] However, as bell hooks and Patricia Hill Collins have recognized, Cooper is among the first to point to the need for black women to articulate their experience from the simultaneous action of racism and patriarchy that determine it (hooks, 1982: 166; Collins, 2002: 37–38). This radical need to engage with the social production of sexual difference allows us to recognize Cooper's adherence to the domestic ideal of womanhood as an antagonistic tactic aimed at challenging the specific subordination prescribed by the masculine and racist definition of womanhood.[39] Cooper honors the "mother-slave" who gave up food in order to send her children to school as "an untrumpeted heroine" whose actions inspire "a new sense of her dignity in the eternal purposes of nature" (Cooper, 1998 [1893]: 203). In this celebration, however, the identification of woman and mother is not simply a replication of the functional order imposed by masculine domination, but crashes against the history of slavery that tore children from their mothers to sell them in the marketplace, and with the racist discourse that views black women as "a *mannerless* sex", making their supposed lack of chastity an attribute of race (Cooper, 1998 [1892]: 96, 48). On the other hand, like others before her, Cooper invokes "mothering influence" (Cooper, 1998 [1892]: 77) and the role it plays in the uplift of the race and the well-being of the individual and the nation in order to claim higher education for the black woman, which was historically considered "a monstrous usurpation of man's prerogative". The invocation of a complementarity between the sexes within a "symmetric whole" (Cooper, 1998 [1892]: 78–79), therefore, has an explicitly polemical

---

37   Cf. Tocqueville, 2002 [1853–1840]: part. 2, ch. 10.
38   Cf. Hubbard, 2009; Lemert, 1998: 14–16. Du Bois quotes Cooper in *The Damnation of Woman* (Du Bois, 1920: 173), without even conceding her the honor of a proper name and speaking only generically of "one of our women". As to the intense correspondence between Cooper and Du Bois, see Moody-Turner, 2015: 47–68.
39   On Cooper's rhetorical strategies, see May, 2009: 17–34.

value and an anti-hierarchical function which defeats the ideological opposition between education and marriage and the consequent condemnation, typically Victorian, of the so-called *surplus women*, or unmarried women (Cooper, 1898).[40] At the same time, it serves to claim the tools for getting out of the poverty that is inherited from the past, from the impossibility of accumulating what Cooper calls "social wealth", a cultural capital made up of books, dictionaries, paintings, and musical instruments, which are the heritage not only of the individual but also of his or her community, and allow each child to make the most of education and free himself and herself and the race from the legacy of the white man (Cooper, 1898).[41]

Cooper also adopts an antagonistic tactic when she makes the Black Woman the privileged subject of a more advanced civilization against American civilization. In its movement – which goes from East to West, as it was for Hegel[42] – civilization sprouts in Europe and blossoms in America, in an overwhelming contrast between Christianity and Islam, between the vigor and movement of Western society and the stasis of Eastern society, most prominently represented by the lotus feet that immobilize and subjugate Chinese women (Cooper, 1998 [1892]: 53). While wholeheartedly embracing the ideology of "manifest destiny", however, Cooper exposes the internal contradictions of American civilization. When the Black Woman voices her experience of rape, male violence becomes an indicator of underdevelopment to the point that many parts of America appear like malaria-infested African jungles (Cooper, 1998 [1892]: 93). When the Black Woman speaks, the domestic space also becomes the site of a "struggle for existence" in which she must assert herself as a worker, claiming the right to independently dispose of a share of her husband's wage, as her work in the home has allowed him to earn a daily income outside the home (Cooper, 1898). When the Black Woman looks at America, she sees the racism that organizes not only the labor market, but also the working-class struggle. Cooper's hostility to anarchism, socialism, and communism is not only an expression of her evolutionary and therefore anti-revolutionary attitude (Cooper, 1998 [1892]: 132), but also of her perception that, while Blacks are put to work as Blacks – at lower wages, in the constant difficulty of finding rents within their reach – the early union organizations and initiatives in northern cities do not fight racism but reproduce it (Cooper, 1998 [1892]: 171, 173).

Still far from the factory, Cooper thinks of free work not as exploitation, but as the source of all wealth, as the possibility to enjoy the fruits of one's activity,

---

40   On *surplus women* in the Victorian context, see Ferrari, 2017: ch. 1.
41   On the weight of "cultural capital" in social reproduction, see Bourdieu, 1987 [1979].
42   Cf. Consolati, 2018: 267–284.

to realize oneself as a self-made man, or woman. This individualism, however, is for her always internal to a process of liberation that can only be collective. For this reason, while the first part of *A Voice from the South* is introduced with an epigraph that announces it as the solo of a "soprano obligato", the second part leaves room for "tutti ad libitum" (Cooper, 1998 [1892]: 50, 120). The Black Woman does not simply speak for herself, but for her entire race and nation. The fact of being 'unrepresentable' – of expressing an absolutely partial position – makes her capable of becoming the only possible representative of all blacks, of all women, of all those who are in one way or another oppressed and aspire to emancipation. Resuming and surpassing Martin R. Delany, according to whom when a black man enters the king's council the whole black race would enter with him, Cooper asserts that

> Only the BLACK WOMAN can say "when and where I enter, in the quiet, undisputed dignity of my womanhood, without violence and without suing or special patronage, then and there the whole Negro race enters with me".
>
> COOPER, 1998 [1892]: 63

Because women's cause is the "cause of the weak" (Cooper, 1998 [1892]: 105), when she gets the consideration she deserves and her own rights, Indians, Blacks, and all who are subjugated will also get their rights. Her epic tells of a historical oppression in which every existing form of oppression converges, pointing to the need to think about how racism has reconfigured masculine domination and how it sustains both social production and reproduction. The Black Woman is not only the general signifier of oppression, but the universal signifier of liberation, which is why she finally becomes Woman *tout court*, once again declined in the singular: "It is not the intelligent woman vs. the ignorant woman; nor the white woman vs. the black, the brown and the red, – it is not even the cause of woman vs. man". Her cause is "linked with that of every agony that has been dumb – every wrong that needs a voice" (Cooper, 1998 [1892]: 107) and for this reason "it is one and universal" (Cooper, 1998 [1902]: 205). While it has the claim to express, without denying them and reproducing them as hierarchies, all the differences starting from the experience of the Black Woman, the concept of woman becomes the synonym of the whole of humanity, the name of a part that advances the claim to illuminate, and finally resolve, every antagonism.

4   The Woman in the Social Factory

In 1892, when Cooper sends *A Voice from the South* to the presses, Emma
Goldman plans a bombing attack in New York. With her partner Aleksandr
Berkman, she wants to kill the steel magnate Henry Clay Frick. He had
responded to the wage demands of his workers by hiring three hundred soldiers, who then fired on the striking crowd and killed sixteen people. The
assembly of the bomb, however, fails, and Goldman decides to prostitute herself in order to get the money to buy a gun. The decision requires courage,
and she takes it from her dedication to the working-class cause. She sews the
clothes she will wear on the street herself, putting the trade she learned in
the textile factory – where she had worked ten hours a day upon her arrival
in the United States from Lithuania – to work against a master. On July 16,
Goldman hits the sidewalk on Fourteenth Street and at the first contact with a
customer she runs away. Eventually she is approached by an older and surprising man who, after asking her a few questions about her first experience on the
street, leaves her ten dollars without asking for anything in return. With that
money she buys the gun that, instead of killing Frick, sends Berkman to jail for
fourteen years (Goldman, 2006 [1931]: ch. 8).[43] All that remains for Goldman
is to continue organizing the struggle against the state and the capitalists, to
inflame the working masses with her exceptional capacity as an agitator and
to question – without ever really coming to terms with – the meaning and
effectiveness of individual action and political violence against the agents of
social violence.

Goldman experiences social violence under the sign of "wage slavery", different from that known by Sojourner Truth and blacks in the South, to whose
specific oppression, as well as racism, she devotes little attention.[44] Instead,
Goldman returns to making slavery into a metaphor, but one capable of forcing millions of men and women to work to reproduce nothing more than their
subsistence. An anarchist and feminist militant, Goldman looks at the factory
from the society it shapes: in her reflection, woman is a concept full of polemical content because it expresses both a masculine domination that capital has
made fully societal, as well as a revolutionary claim of liberation. The experience of sexual oppression cannot be separated from the conditions in which it is
determined, and for this very reason prostitution – which she had encountered

---

43   About this episode see Leroy, 2014: 37 ff. For a review of biographical studies on Goldman,
      cf. Wheeling 2007.

44   On Goldman and the problem of race, see Hemmings, 2018: ch.2. The volume contains the
      most up-to-date review of the writings about Goldman.

by political choice, but which had taken on unprecedented dimensions in the United States at the turn of the century (Goldman, 1910: 190) – illuminates the systematic relationship between patriarchy and capitalism and the way it operates within political and social institutions. Goldman's working-class perspective questions the idea that it is possible to free oneself from sexual oppression without struggling against the capital that extracts value from it. At the same time, capitalist society cannot be destroyed without demolishing the sexed conditions of its reproduction. As a signifier of the irreducible social determination of sexual difference, the concept of woman is always and nec-essarily revealed to be internally split precisely because it is subjected to the contradictions of the social factory. Therefore, at the moment in which women become fundamental figures of the industrial system, the universalistic ten-sion that in the second half of the nineteenth century had characterized the discourse of their emancipation is confronted with the challenge of a concrete condition that is explicitly polemical towards the abstract discourse of rights embraced by the suffragists. The battle for free love, contraception, and free motherhood becomes the focus of a revolutionary ambition that does not aim to find a place for women in the existing society, because it claims to over-throw it.

Goldman considers prostitution a "social factor" (Goldman, 1910: 199) because its growth between the nineteenth and twentieth centuries is linked to the development of industry, the entry of the masses into the free labor market and its competitive nature, employment instability, and urban overcrowding around large factories. What causes the trade in women of all colors is exploita-tion, "the merciless Moloch of capitalism that fattens on underpaid labor, thus driving thousands of women and girls into prostitution" (Goldman, 1910: 184). Even if it is an "ancient evil" – as Jane Addams, one of the main exponents of the settlement houses movement, defined it (Addams, 1912)[45] – prostitution must be understood in relation to the "spirit of our commercial age" and to wage labor (Goldman, 1910: 199). Prostitutes are mainly workers, often married, who sell their bodies to cope with periods of unemployment and supplement family incomes that are insufficient even for survival. However, it is not only a matter of necessity: prostitution can be a way of escaping from the constraints imposed by the wage, an "outlet" for those who are treated as "drudges", a way to obtain the necessary resources to buy clothes to integrate into American society, where elegance is always ostentatious (Goldman, 1910: 187).

---

45   On the experience of social work and settlement houses see Baritono, 2002 and Bianchi, 2004.

Economic necessity and the aspiration to have something more than mere survival establish a continuity between prostitution and marriage, which institutionalizes "the sovereignty of the man over the woman, ... and absolute dependence on his name and support" (Goldman, 1910: 227). Marriage is a "life insurance" (Goldman, 1910: 234), the result of a calculation, a choice forced both by need – which drives women to give their bodies to a man in a regime of "monopoly" in exchange for subsistence – and by the desire to escape the prison of the factory by relying on a husband and his income. In the case of working-class women, however, this hope is mostly in vain, so that they will be forced to move from the "prison" of the factory to the "prison" of the home, where domestic work compounds the burden of wage slavery (Goldman, 1910: 239). Working-class and middle-class women – trained to believe that getting married is their "goal" – are thus united by the "fetish of the home" and by the bond with a "domestic sphere" created by man for his own exclusive benefit to make them wives, mothers, and servants (Goldman, 1910: 191, 202). Working-class and middle-class women are not equal, however, because it is only the former who are forced to work for a living. Treating prostitution as a social factor, then, Goldman makes the prostitute a working-class figure – because she works in a factory, or because she has no access to property – and also recognizes that the relationship with property determines the different intensity and productive function of sexual oppression.

Between the production of wealth and sex there is a relationship that can no longer be ignored. Sex is an instrument of labor discipline because it responds to the sexual demand around factories and production sites and because it determines the specific way women can enter the market. It also influences the conditions of their access to social wealth, the equally specific way in which they fight to win wage and against its misery, and the position in which they are placed in the sexual and social division of labor. In a world in which every master is convinced that he can also demand sexual services from his female workers, even their possibility of earning more than mere subsistence may depend on the use of their bodies, the only bargaining chip they have in the market "to keep a position in whatever field". The prostitute illuminates the sexed character of every manifestation of capitalist domination. Because she is a "a product of social conditions", her liberation depends on the ability to interrupt the process of producing women as "sex commodities" (Goldman, 1910: 185, 200, 190).

Goldman thinks of sex within the "relentless and bloody battle" between the individual and society, in which the latter stifles the instincts of the former. The need for sexual gratification is part of these instincts, it is "natural" and could be satisfied freely, but this does not and should not happen (Goldman, 1910: 57,

64). Morality assumes a prominent role precisely because of its regulatory function of instincts, showing that the "individual" to which Goldman refers is not a neutral subject, but is instead sexually differentiated, and this determines the intensity of the social coercion he or she undergoes. Puritanism in fact imposes a double moral code: it allows men to have their own sexual experiences, even to frequent brothels, because it considers those experiences as part of their "general development", while it brands any woman who practices sex outside of marriage with a "scarlet letter" (Goldman, 1910: 191, 173).[46] According to this code, women are "oversexed" (Goldman, 1910: 178), meaning that they are treated as sexual objects, literally identified with sex and simultaneously left in total ignorance as to its importance. Puritan morality thus establishes an asymmetry between women and men that is functional to the reproduction of industrial capitalism. Sex is the ever-denied supplement to what Max Weber called "worldly asceticism" (Weber, 2001 [1905]: 53 ff.), a discipline of labor and a rationalization of instincts that can be attributed to men because the economic irrationality proper to the drive for immediate enjoyment is treated as specifically feminine. At the same time, the "narrow spirit" of Puritanism (Goldman, 1910: 173) economizes the woman's need for sexual gratification by subjecting it to masculine domination, both when it forces her to postpone its satisfaction in view of marriage, and when it pushes her into prostitution to atone for a sexual experience deemed illicit. The over-sexualization that results from man's social symbolic labor is configured as a form of expropriation: since for Goldman property corresponds to a "domination over the body" and "human needs" (Goldman, 1910: 68, 59) that denies those who are dominated the right to satisfy them, the repression of female sexual desire transforms the woman's body into a commodity that opposes her as an alien power, determines her position in the market, and defines the legitimate space of her movements. The signification of the concept of woman in the context of early American industrial capitalism shows that the latter reproduces itself through the constant production of masculine domination.

The prostitute, the wife and the mother are all figures of this same process of social production, within which they occupy different positions but made equivalent by the code of masculine domination and its capitalist valorization. The "Property Morality" makes the institution that produces poverty and pushes the poor to have awe and respect for their masters into something "sacred" (Goldman, 1998 [1913a]: 170). Along with the "Family Morality", it contributes to the creation of the prostitute – imposing on her the guilt of experiencing sex

---

46   Goldman clearly refers to Nathaniel Hawthorne's well-known novel, published in 1850.

outside the spaces regulated by masculine domination – and a mother incapable of being a mother, who ignores her own sexuality and yet is obligated to
procreate. While economic dependence gives wealth the power to command
labor by transforming men into the "particle of a machine" (Goldman, 1910: 60),
the oversexualization of women determines both the masculine economy of
her desire and the specific ways in which capitalist command is exercised
inside and outside the factory. The definition of the woman as a sexual object
is not a novelty of the twentieth century, but industrial capitalism subdues that
definition to its own logic, redetermining its societal function. By criticizing
the social process that establishes the content of the concept of woman in the
early twentieth-century United States, Goldman brings to light what Weberian
sociology of religion leaves in the shadows, namely the patriarchal character of
the Protestant ethic that sustains the spirit of capitalism.

Like Wollstonecraft and Cooper before her, Goldman confronts a process
that produces its own subjects, a discipline that institutes the paradoxical
acceptance by individuals of their subjection. This explains her retrieval of
the "brutal" Nietzschean maxim "You go to women? Do not forget the whip!"
(Goldman, 1910: 201; Nietzsche 2007 [1883–1885]: 50),[47] which allows her to
indict the fervent support that women themselves offer to the Christian religion that enslaved them, fully manifest in the campaigns of Moral Reform
promoted by the feminist movement during the 1800s and culminating in
the 1910s and 1920s. Goldman loves Nietzsche very much but is inevitably
forced to distance herself from the nationalistic implications of his philosophy (Goldman, 1998 [1915]: 214–215) and his exaltation of the "master morality"
(Goldman, 1998 [1913b]: 238). Yet she believes that he should not be treated as
a "social theorist", but rather as "a poet, a rebel, an innovator" (Goldman, 2006
[1931]: 126), who together with Max Stirner shed light on the way in which the
"slave morality" generates and perpetuates a "slavery of the spirit". Not only is
this "a premium on parasitism and inertia" (Goldman, 1998 [1913b]: 232–33) by
denying life and all that gives strength to character, it also takes the form of an
ideology whose effectiveness consists in the constant production of an exception aimed at legitimizing what exists as a norm. Thus, for example, in the face
of the great scandal aroused by the "procurer" of prostitutes, singled out by
society as criminals, the owners of department stores and factories who every
day reduce women to misery by pushing them into the street "enjoy immunity
and respect" (Goldman, 1910: 198). By condemning a pocket of crime and guilt
as excess, public morality legitimizes the normality of masculine domination

---

47   On Goldman and Nietzsche, see Ferguson, 2007 and Rossdale, 2015.

and capitalist exploitation by decreeing their necessity in the minds of those who are dominated and exploited. This dynamic has a fundamental function in the legitimation of the state, as the slave morality crushes "the natural impulse of the primitive man to strike back, to avenge a wrong", so that he is driven to delegate the task of doing so to an "organized machinery" (Goldman, 1910: 124). There is a constitutive analogy between faith in God and the legitimation of the state, since the authority of both is supported by the "dogma" of a negative anthropology that makes man a being "vicious and too incompetent to know what is good for him" (Goldman, 1998 [1940]: 113), prompting him to forgo action. As is the case in Nietzsche, for Goldman the state is also a "cold monster" that crushes individuality by presenting itself as a "new idol" (Goldman, 1940: 117; Nietzsche 2007 [1883–1835]: 34). Her genealogy of morals therefore requires the proclamation of the death of God and the untying of feminism from the political theology that it has historically used against masculine domination, but which now turns out to be a way to legitimize authority by imposing the alternative between the norm and its exception.

The working-class perspective and the critique of Puritan morality clarify Goldman's polemic with suffragist feminism, which does not pose the problem of interrupting the social processes of the production of women as sexual commodities, but takes part in them thinking it can give those processes another form. The claim of women's suffrage aims to obtain equal rights in every social sphere and is linked to the defense of the right to property and the claim of its political recognition. However, Goldman asks, "what avail is that right to the mass of women without property?" (Goldman, 1910: 207). While the condition of the working-class woman forces us to think about the way in which capitalist society puts masculine domination at the service of its own reproduction, the movement for emancipation – the term by which Goldman defines the struggle for suffrage – is the expression of the "American woman of the middle class" who from her position can indeed see and challenge her own sexual oppression, but fails to recognize the privileges that derive from the "economic superiority" she enjoys, which will only be increased by the attainment of the right to vote. Seeing work as a "just provision of providence" (Goldman, 1910: 212–214), legitimizing the existence of the poor for the benefit of the rich, the suffragist movement has been hostile to workers' struggles, when it has not obstructed them. With a few exceptions – including militant English suffragism led by Sylvia Pankhurst, which combined a claim to the vote with a struggle for wages and direct action[48] – the suffragist movement conceives of

---

48   On Sylvia Pankhurst, see Winslow, 1996.

women as one-dimensional because it fails to address the social determination of their oppression – the way access to property re-signifies sexed experience – and thus ends up reproducing the exclusive identification of woman and sex that supports masculine domination.

Affirming the perspective of the working woman thus requires Goldman to take note of the way social power operates within institutions. If the state is the "organized authority" for the sole purpose of "protecting property and monopoly" (Goldman, 1910: 213), then access to political rights cannot modify or compensate for the social inequalities determined by property. The state is not a neutral instance. It is the guarantor of capitalist and masculine domination, which it institutionalizes through, for example, laws prohibiting strikes or punishing prostitutes or imposing fines and levies on them that intensify their exposure to sexual exploitation. In Goldman's critique of suffragism, the working woman becomes the impossible subject of rights, showing the inner limits of a discourse indifferent to the material condition she experiences in the capitalist industrial enterprise. The suffragist movement has indeed succeeded in eradicating the idea that woman is merely a "domestic drudge" (Goldman, 1910: 216). However, in the era of industrial free labor her oppression leaves servitude behind and is rearticulated according to the logic of exploitation. Like black women and men subjugated by racism after the end of slavery, working-class women make it clear that emancipation does not immediately entail the overthrow of masculine domination and property, which through emancipation continues to determine different access to social power for individuals, both men and women. By granting women an equal right to be represented, suffrage would give them the opportunity to participate in the defense of property, the institution that imposes an emancipation achieved under the pressure of economic necessity on most of them, i.e., the right to be exploited as much as and more than men. The working woman therefore recognizes the homologating logic of American democracy – a "clumsy attempt ... to regulate the complexities of human character by means of external equality" (Goldman, 1998 [1915]: 215) – revealing the fracture that cuts American democracy in two and the impossibility of welding it through the extension of rights.

When she states that "woman is confronted with the necessity of emancipating herself from emancipation, if she really desires to be free", Goldman knows she is exposing herself to the risk of being referred to as "an opponent of women" (Goldman, 1910: 221, 215). She herself, however, must recognize that emancipation is part of a process of liberation and cannot be dismissed as a continuation of the subjugation of women through integration into the system that oppresses them. Sixty years after the Seneca Falls Convention, [woman] has molded a new atmosphere and a new life for herself. She has become a world-power in every domain of human thought and activity. And all that without suffrage, without the right to make laws, without the privilege' of becoming a judge, a jailer, or an executioner.

GOLDMAN, 1910: 216

In the war between society and the individual, the emancipationist movement allowed women to assert the natural and creative instincts denied by the state and God. The freedom they thus practiced is not merely negative, the absence of external constraints, but is an inner liberation that coincides with the "power to achieve freedom" (Goldman, 1910: 225). Freedom is the practice of a transformation of oneself and what exists, and in fact, precisely when they have struggled to define themselves autonomously outside the limits imposed by the one-sided definition of their position – for example, by practicing divorce, abortion and contraception even against the law – women have operated as a "world-power" delegitimizing masculine domination.

This power, however, risked being stifled once again by the moralism that characterized the suffragist movement since the Seneca Falls *Declaration of Sentiments*, which had claimed the right to vote for women on the basis of their supposed moral superiority and the beneficial effects it would have on corrupt male politics. Goldman acknowledges the antagonistic tactics used to advance the feminist battle by circumventing the charges of debauchery leveled against the women's movement by its detractors, who were always concerned with disciplining the diseconomy of female desire. The tactic, however, ends up thwarting the strategy: first of all, it replicates the alternative between norm and exception, because it sees corruption as a crime, rather than the ordinary reflection "of business and industrial world" (Goldman, 1910: 221), and entrusts the state with the task of healing society's injustices. Second, it tightens the grip of Puritan patriarchalism not only on the middle-class women of whom the movement is an expression, but also on the working-class women who, because of the promiscuity of factory work, have a more direct relationship with their sexual desires (Goldman, 1910: 192; 1998 [1913a]: 173). The slave morality that subjugates women must be overthrown through an "eternal yes to life" like the one pronounced by Zarathustra, and it is in this perspective that sex becomes for Goldman a central terrain for the feminist struggle. It is not a principle of women's identification, but the breaking point of the identity subdued to the logics of masculine and capitalist domination that operate in the social production of their difference:

The defenders of authority dread the advent of a free motherhood, lest it will rob them of their prey. Who would fight wars? Who would create wealth? Who would make the policeman, the jailer, if woman were to refuse the indiscriminate breeding of children? The race, the race! shouts the king, the president, the capitalist, the priest. The race must be preserved ... Woman no longer wants to be a party to the production of a race of ... human beings, who have neither the strength nor moral courage to throw off the yoke of poverty and slavery.

GOLDMAN, 1910: 182

The "mother instinct" and the "innate craving for motherhood" (Goldman, 1910: 223, 225) invoked by Goldman in support of the free choice to become mothers should not be understood as an irresponsible replication of the constant masculine identification of women with their presumed biological destiny. On the contrary, they are a manifestation of the revolt of the individual against the species, which justifies the feminist use of Nietzsche against Spencerian evolutionism, guilty of legitimizing – starting from the identification between what is "good" and what is "useful" – both the subordination of women by virtue of their procreative function, and the "commercial spirit" of the time. The "perfect functioning of the regulating unconscious instincts" invoked by Nietzsche (Nietzsche 1989 [1887]: 27, 39) against the 'anti-natural' character of modern society[49] becomes for Goldman a weapon against the process of discipline that supports the subjection of women to masculine domination and the subjection of workers – men and women – to capital. The valorization of the maternal instinct against the societal discipline explains the militancy in favor of contraception and against the criminalization of abortion, a militancy which for years Goldman had committed together with the feminist Margaret Sanger.[50] Motherhood can be free only if the love that makes it mature as a choice is free, and this means tearing down marriage, the institution *par excellence* of masculine domination. On the other hand, free love – which Goldman herself practiced while living her life and which, starting from the end of the nineteenth century, had become in the United States the claim of many women and feminists linked to cooperative and utopian experiences[51] – is possible only if a woman knows herself, if she takes back what has been taken away from her by overturning the social process of

49   On the lexicon of instincts, Haaland, 1993 and Orsucci, 1992: 171 ff.
50   On the relationship between Goldman and Sanger in the birth control initiative, Drinnon, 1967: 210 ff.
51   Cf. Stoehr, 1977.

expropriation that has reduced her to a mere object of male sexual enjoyment. It is not just a matter of conquering individual sovereignty over one's own person by invoking that Lockean self-ownership that legitimizes property as an institution and, with it, wage slavery.[52] Free love is a feminist practice against property because it aims to overthrow both the moral system that supports it and the authorities that defend and impose it with the violence of law and exploitation. Free motherhood and free love are practices through which, by transforming herself, woman transforms the social conditions of her production as a sexual commodity.

Feminism is configured in this way as a cut, as an affirmation of self that coincides with the refusal of the woman "to be a servant to God, the State, society, the husband, the family" (Goldman, 1910: 217). In this light, Goldman's clash with Marxism, even more than with Marx (Goldman, 1998 [1940]: 122),[53] is not simply the foregone conclusion of her anarchism, which moreover was strengthened by the period of exile she spent in Soviet Russia and the Kronstadt massacre she had witnessed and tried to avoid (Goldman, 1923). Her problem is to find a way out of the totalizing dimension of societal domination, the way it continuously produces and reproduces its subjects, making it impossible to think of the revolution as the necessary outcome of the same conditions of which we must be free. The Nietzschean lexicon of instincts is reflected in Goldman's peculiar politics of life, in an appeal to nature that coincides with a condition that is not pre-social, but anti-societal, with a positive anthropology that trusts in the presence of a "living force in the affairs of our life, constantly creating new conditions" (Goldman, 1910: 73) which is already present and can never be completely repressed. This politics of life – which is articulated in an organicism that is expressly polemical towards the mechanism of the modern state – should finally allow a reconciliation between individual instincts, necessary for any innovation, and social instincts, which determine "mutual helpfulness", a propensity for cooperation to be asserted against society and the capitalist logic of competition. Revolution can be conceived as "thought carried into action" (Goldman, 1910: 73) precisely because it expresses an instinct that is alive in every individual and cannot be suppressed. The revolutionary meaning of sexual freedom consists, therefore, in being the practice of an inner freedom that is already present, yet silent, to which woman gives voice when she rejects the social conditions that enjoin her silence.

---

52   Cf. Macpherson, 2010 [1973]: 225–296.

53   Where she recognizes that the Marxist "has outmarxed Marx himself".

For Goldman, those conditions are always and simultaneously masculine domination and capital: in order for the prostitute to be able to speak, it is necessary to fight for a "complete transvaluation of all accepted values ... coupled with the abolition of industrial slavery" (Goldman, 1910: 200), a movement "beyond good and evil" that is essential to the struggle against capitalist domination because it makes possible the "spirit of rebellion" and direct action (Goldman, 1910: 68), both individual and collective, against exploitation. In this movement, the universalistic tension expressed in the concept of woman is charged with concreteness. Goldman's admiration for Mary Wollstonecraft is linked to her ability to be "untimely" – as Nietzsche had defined every effort made to generate something new (Nietzsche 1997 [1873–1876]: 60) – and to her claim as a woman not only the freedom of her sex but that of the entire human race (Goldman, 1998 [1914]: 224; 1981 [1911]: 116).[54] Like Wollstonecraft, Goldman also views woman as an "artificial being" to whom society has denied the possibility of "being human". However, for Wollstonecraft this humanity could be achieved only by recognizing woman as an individual entitled with rights, the figure *par excellence* of the modern political universal, and therefore by abstraction from both sex and its social determination. For Goldman, on the contrary, individual "rights" are "abstraction derived from the non-reality known as 'the State'" (Goldman 1998 [1940]: 121). The individual entitled with rights is therefore itself an abstraction and at the same time a figure of domination, as the "rugged individualism" invoked by Hoover at the end of 1928 to face the Great Depression has made evident (Hoover, 1928), an individualism "for the masters" destined to sustain the American market economy against European socialist paternalism (Goldman, 1998 [1940]: 121).

The individuality that Goldman invokes against society and its state is instead concrete and embodied. It coincides with the practice of freedom, which is why the woman who struggles against the social conditions of her subordination is "a force hitherto unknown in the world" that carries with it a promise of "real love, peace, and harmony" (Goldman, 1910: 217). This struggle does not have the aim of "'harmonizing' the most antagonistic elements in society", as is the case for the agents of the modern political universal: "laws, police, soldiers, the courts, legislatures, prisons" (Goldman, 1910: 65). On the contrary, it practices a "general social antagonism" which should be overcome in a "perfect whole" in which all differences of class and race, and between man and woman, can be reunified without "the elimination of individual traits and peculiarities" (Goldman, 1910: 219). Goldman, like Cooper, eventually

---

54   On Goldman and Wollstonecraft, see Wexler, 2007.

foreshadows the possibility of a symphonic order in which every note can resonate, giving meaning to the whole. Unlike Cooper, however, she does not think that this should happen according to the score of existing society. At the heart of capitalist society, as emancipation continues – despite Goldman's critique – to fuel feminism as a liberation movement, the concept of woman highlights the point of maximum tension in the modern universal, which clashes with the practice and possibility of revolutionary difference. This difference, embodied by the working woman, expresses a universalist tension not because it abstracts from differences and the social conditions of their production, but because it challenges those conditions and points to the possibility that all differences can speak without being crushed and silenced by the homogenizing force of the modern political universal, of masculine domination and capital.

References

Adams, A. (1875) *Familiar Letters of John Adams and His Wife Abigail Adams, during the Revolution*. Boston – New York: Houghton Mifflin Company.

Addams, J. (1912) *A New Conscience and an Ancient Evil*. New York: Macmillan.

Alexander, E. (1995) "We Must Be about Our Father's Business": Anna Julia Cooper and the In-Corporation of the Nineteenth-Century African-American Woman Intellectual. *Signs* 2: 336–356.

Alridge, D.P. (2007) Of Victorianism, Civilizationism and Progressivism: The Educational Ideas of Anna Julia Cooper and W.E.B. Du Bois, 1892–1940. *History of Education Quarterly* 4: 416–446.

Baritono, R. (2001) Introduzione. In: Baritono R. (ed) *Il sentimento delle libertà. La Dichiarazione di Seneca Falls e il dibattito sui diritti delle donne negli Stati Uniti di metà Ottocento*. Torino: La Rosa, VII–LXXIV.

Baritono, R. (2002) Infrangere le barriere: donne, sfera pubblica e sfera politica negli Stati Uniti nell'Ottocento e nel Novecento. In: Gherardi R. (ed) *Politica, consenso, legittimità. Trasformazioni e prospettive*. Roma: Carocci, 155–176.

Battistini, M. (2022) *Middle Class. An Intellectual History through Social Sciences. An American Fetish from Its Origins to Globalization*. Leiden – Boston: Brill.

Beauvoir, S. de (1956 [1949]) *The Second Sex*. London: Jonathan Cape.

Beecher, C.E. (1835) *An Essay on Slavery and Abolitionism, with Reference to the Duty of American Females*. Philadelphia: Perkins&Marvin.

Bergès, S. and Coffee, A. (2016) (eds) *The Social and Political Philosophy of Mary Wollstonecraft*. Oxford: Oxford University Press.

Bianchi, B. (2004) Il pensiero sociale di Jane Addams (1881–1916). In: Addams J. (2004) *Donne, immigrati, governo della città. Scritti sull'etica sociale.* Bianchi B. (ed). Santa Maria Capua a Vetere: Spartaco, 7–67.

Bourdieu, P. (1987 [1979]) *Distinction. A Social Critique of the Judgement of Taste.* Cambridge (MS): Harvard University Press.

Bourdieu, P. (2001 [1998]) *Masculine Domination.* Stanford: Stanford University Press.

Burke, E. (1999 [1790]) Reflections on the Revolution in France. In: Burke E. (1999) *Select Works of Edmund Burke*, vol. 2. Indianapolis: Liberty Fund.

Cady Stanton, E. (1981 [1882]) The Solitude of Self. In: DuBois E.C. (ed) *Elizabeth Cady Stanton and Susan B. Anthony: Correspondence, Writings, and Speeches.* New York: Schocken Books, 246–254.

Casadei, T. (2016) Sarah Moore Grimké: le radici bibliche dell'argomentazione femminista. In: Grimké S.M., *Poco meno degli angeli. Lettere sull'uguaglianza dei sessi.* Roma: Castelvecchi, 5–15.

Casalini, B. (2008) "Only the philosophical eye". La Rivoluzione francese nella lettura di Mary Wollstonecraft. *Filosofia Politica* 2: 195–218.

Child, L.M (1835) *The History of the Condition of Women, in Various Ages and Nations.* Boston: John Allen & Co.

Collins, P. (2002) *Black Feminist Thought: Knowledge, Consciousness, and the Politics of Empowerment.* London: Taylor & Francis.

Consolati, I. (2018) Tra il globo e lo Stato. Storia e politica del concetto di spazio in Germania tra Settecento e Ottocento. *Filosofia Politica* 2: 267–284.

Cooper, A.J. (1898) Colored Women as Wage-Earners. *The Southern Workman* 28(8): 295–298.

Cooper, A.J. (1998 [1892]) A Voice from the South. In: Lemert C. and Bhan E. (eds) *The Voice of Anna Julia Cooper.* Lanham – Boulder – New York – Toronto – Oxford: Rowman & Littlefield, 45–196.

Cooper, A.J. (1998 [1893]) The Intellectual Progress of the Colored Women in the United States since the Emancipation Proclamation: A Response to Fannie Barrier Williams. In: Lemert C. and Bhan E. (eds) *The Voice of Anna Julia Cooper.* Lanham – Boulder – New York – Toronto – Oxford: Rowman & Littlefield, 201–205.

Cooper, A.J. (1998 [1902]) The Ethics of the Negro Question. In: Lemert C. and Bhan E. (eds) *The Voice of Anna Julia Cooper.* Lanham – Boulder – New York – Toronto – Oxford: Rowman & Littlefield, 206–215.

Cooper, A.J. (1998 [1913]) Social Settlement: What is it and What it does. In: Lemert C. and Bhan E. (eds) *The Voice of Anna Julia Cooper.* Lanham – Boulder – New York – Toronto – Oxford: Rowman & Littlefield, 216–235.

Cossutta, C. (2017) Educare come gesto politico. La riflessione di Mary Wollstonecraft. *Storia del pensiero politico* 2: 197–222.

de Gouges, O. (1986 [1791]) *Dèclaration des droits de la femme et de la citoyenne*. In: de Gouges O. (1986) *Œuvres*. Groult B. (ed). Paris: Mercure de France, 101–112.

de Gouges, O. (1792) Invitation aux dames françaises, pour la fête du maire d'Etampes. In: de Gouges O. (1792) *Lettres à la Reine, aux Généraux de l'Armée, aux Amis de la Constitution, et aux Françaises citoyennes. Description de la fête du 3 juin, par Marie-Olympe de Gouges.* Paris: Société typographique aux Jacobins Saint-Honoré, 11–13.

Degler, C.N. (1991) *In Search of Human Nature. The Decline and Revival of Darwinism in American Social Thought.* New York – Oxford: Oxford University Press.

Douglass, F. (1992 [1883]) Parties were Made for Men, Not Men for Parties. In: Blassingame J.W. and McKivigan J.R. (eds) *The Frederick Douglass Papers*, vol. 5. New Haven: Yale University Press, 85–110.

Drinnon, R. (1967) *Rebel in Paradise: A Biography of Emma Goldman.* Chicago: University of Chicago Press.

Du Bois, W.E.B. (1897) Strivings of the Negro People. *Atlantic Monthly* 478: 194–198.

Du Bois, W.E.B. (1920) *Darkwater. Voices from within the Veil.* New York: Harcourt, Brace and Howe.

DuBois, E.C. (1998) *Woman Suffrage and Women's Rights.* New York – London: New York University Press.

Ferguson, K.E. (2007) Religion, Faith, and Politics. Reading Goldman Through Nietzsche. In: Weiss P.A. and Kensinger L. (eds) *Feminist Interpretations of Emma Goldman.* University Park: The Pennsylvania State University Press, 92–107.

Ferguson, S. (1999) The Radical Ideas of Mary Wollstonecraft. *Canadian Journal of Political Science* 3: 427–450.

Ferrari, R. (2017) *Beatrice Potter e il capitalismo senza civiltà. Una donna tra scienza, politica e amministrazione.* Roma: Viella.

Foner, E. (1998) *The Story of American Freedom.* New York – London: W.W. Norton.

General Association of Massachusetts (2000 [1837]) Pastoral Letter to Churches under Their Care. In: Sklar K.K. (ed) *Women's Rights Emerges within the Antislavery Movement. 1830–1870. A Brief History with Documents.* Boston: Palgrave MacMillan, 119–121.

Godineau, D. (1988) *Citoyennes tricoteuses: les femmes du peuple a Paris pendant la Revolution francaise.* Aix-en-Provence: Alinea.

Goldman, E. (1910) *Anarchism and Other Essays.* New York: Mother Earth Publishing Association.

Goldman, E. (1923) *My Disillusionment in Russia.* New York: Doubleday, Page & Co.

Goldman, E. (1981 [1911]) Mary Wollstonecraft. Her Tragic Life and Her Passionate Struggle for Freedom. *Feminist Studies* 1: 114–121.

Goldman, E. (1998 [1913a]) Victims of Morality. In: Kates Shulman A. (ed) *Red Emma Speaks. An Emma Goldman Reader.* Amherst – New York: Humanity Books, 168–174.

Goldman, E. (1998 [1913b]) The Failure of Christianity. In: Kates Shulman A. (ed) *Red Emma Speaks. An Emma Goldman Reader*. Amherst – New York: Humanity Books, 231–240.

Goldman, E. (1998 [1914]) Intellectual Proletarians. In: Kates Shulman A. (ed), *Red Emma Speaks. An Emma Goldman Reader*. Amherst – New York: Humanity Books, 222–231.

Goldman, E. (1998 [1915]) Jealousy: Causes and a Possible Cure. In: Kates Shulman A. (ed) *Red Emma Speaks. An Emma Goldman Reader*. Amherst – New York: Humanity Books, 214–221.

Goldman, E. (1998 [1940]) The Individual, Society and the State. In: Kates Shulman A. (ed) *Red Emma Speaks. An Emma Goldman Reader*. Amherst – New York: Humanity Books, 109–123.

Goldman, E. (2006 [1931]) *Living My Life*. London: Penguin.

Gordon, L. (2005) *Vindication. A Life of Mary Wollstonecraft*. New York: Harper Collins Publishers.

Grimké, S.M. (1998 [1855]) Marriage. In: Lerner G. (ed) *The Feminist Thought of Sarah Grimké*. New York – Oxford: Oxford University Press, 107–115.

Grimké, S.M. (2014 [1837a]) Letters on the Equality of the Sexes, and the Condition of Woman. In: Grimké S.M. and Grimké A.E. (2014) *On Slavery and Abolitionism. Essays and Letters*. London: Penguin Books, 31–119.

Grimké, S.M. (2014 [1837b]) An Epistle to the Clergy of the Southern States. In: Grimké S.M. and Grimké A.E. (2014) *On Slavery and Abolitionism. Essays and Letters*. London: Penguin Books, 3–30.

Gunther-Canada, W. (1996) Mary Wollstonecraft's "Wild Wish": Confounding Sex in the Discourse of Political Rights. In: Falco M.J. (ed) *Feminist Interpretations of Mary Wollstonecraft*. University Park: The Pennsylvania State University Press, 61–83.

Haaland, B. (1993) *Emma Goldman: Sexuality and the Impurity of the State*. Montreal: Black Rose Book.

Halldenius, L. (2015) *Mary Wollstonecraft and Feminist Republicanism. Independence, Rights and the Experience of Unfreedom*. London: Pickering & Chatto.

Haraway, D. (1992) Ecce Homo, Ain't (Ar'n't) I a Woman, and Inappropriate/d Others: The Human in a Post-Humanist Landscape. In: Butler J. and Scott J.W. (eds) *Feminists Theorize the Political*. New York – London: Routledge, 86–100.

Harper, F.E.W. (1893) Woman's Political Future. In: Sewell M.W. (ed) *World Congress of Representative Women*. New York – Chicago: Rand, McNally & Co, 433–436.

Hawkins, M. (1997) *Social Darwinism in European and American Thought, 1860–1945*. Cambridge: Cambridge University Press.

Hemmings, C. (2018) *Considering Emma Goldman. Feminist Political Ambivalence and Imaginative Archive*. Durham – London: Duke University Press.

hooks, b. (1982) *Ain't I a Woman. Black Women and Feminism.* London-Winchester: Pluto Press.

Hoover, H. (1928) Principles and Ideals of the United States Government. Available (consulted 23 April, 2023) at: https://www.digitalhistory.uh.edu/disp_textbook .cfm?smtID=3&psid=1334.

Hubbard, L.C. (2009) When and Where I Enter: Anna Julia Cooper, Afrocentric Theory, and Africana Studies. *Journal of Black Studies* 2: 283–295.

Hunt Botting, E. (2016) *Wollstonecraft, Mill and Women's Human Rights.* New Haven-London: Yale University Press.

Irigaray, L. (1987 [1974]) *Speculum. Of the Other Woman.* Ithaca (NY): Cornell University Press.

Johnson, K.A. (2000) *Uplifting the Women and the Race. The Educational Philosophies and Social Activism of Anna Julia Cooper and Nannie Helen Burroughs.* New York: Routledge.

Kant, I. (1997 [1785]) *Groundworks of the Metaphysics of Morals.* Cambridge: Cambridge University Press.

Koselleck, R. (2004 [1979]) *Futures Past. On the Semantics of Historical Time.* New York: Columbia University Press.

Laudani, R. (2007) Introduzione. In: Laudani R. (ed) *La libertà a ogni costo. Scritti abolizionisti afroamericani.* Torino: La Rosa, IX–LVIII.

Leddy, N. (2016) Mary Wollstonecraft and Adam Smith on Gender, History and the Civic Republican Tradition. In: Kellow G.C. and Leddy N. (eds) *On Civic Republicanism. Ancient Lessons for Global Politics.* Toronto: University of Toronto Press, 269–281.

Lemert, Ch. (1998) Anna Julia Cooper: The Colored Woman's Office. In: Lemert C. and Bhan E. (eds) *The Voice of Anna Julia Cooper.* Lanham – Boulder – New York – Toronto – Oxford: Rowman & Littlefield, 1–43.

Lerner, G. (1971) *The Grimké Sisters From South Carolina: Pioneers for Women's Rights and Abolition.* New York: Schocken Books.

Lerner, G. (1979) *The Majority Finds Its Past. Placing Women in History.* Oxford: Oxford University Press.

Lerner, G. (1998) Introduction. In: Lerner G. (ed) *The Feminist Thought of Sarah Grimké.* New York – Oxford: Oxford University Press.

Leroy, M. (2014) *Emma Goldman: une éthique de l'émancipation.* Lyon: Atelier de création libertaire.

Macpherson, C.B. (2010 [1973]) *The Political Theory of Possessive Individualism: Hobbes to Locke.* Oxford: Oxford University Press.

Maréchal, S. (1801) *Projet de loi portant défense d'apprendre à lire aux femmes.* Paris: Chez Massé.

May, V.M. (2007) *Anna Julia Cooper, Visionary Black Feminist. A Critical Introduction.* New York – London: Routledge.

May, V.M. (2009) Writing the Self into Being: Anna Julia Cooper's Textual Politics. *African American Review* 43/1: 17–34.

Michelet, J. (1855 [1854]) *The Women of the French Revolution.* Philadelphia: Henry Carey Baird.

Moody-Turner, S. (2015) "Dear Doctor Du Bois": Anna Julia Cooper, W.E.B. Du Bois, and the Gender Politics of Black Publishing. *Melus* 3: 47–68.

Morrison, T. (1987) *Beloved.* New York: Alfred A. Knopf Inc.

Nietzsche, F. (1989 [1887]) On the Genealogy of Morals. A Polemical Writing. In: Kauffman W. (ed) *On the Genealogy of Morals and Ecce Homo.* New York: Vintage Book, 15–200.

Nietzsche, F. (1997 [1873–1876]) *Untimely Meditations.* Breazeale D. and Hollingdale R.J. (eds). Cambridge: Cambridge University Press.

Nietzsche, F. (2007 [1883–1885]) *Thus Spoke Zarathustra. A Book for All and None.* Del Caro A. and Pippin R.B. (eds). Cambridge: Cambridge University Press.

O'Neill, D.I. (2007) *The Burke-Wollstonecraft Debate: Savagery, Civilization, and Democracy.* University Park: The Pennsylvania State University Press.

Orsucci, A. (1992) *Dalla biologia cellulare alle scienze dello spirito. Aspetti del dibattito sull'individualità nell'Ottocento tedesco.* Bologna: Il Mulino.

Pateman, C. (2003 [1980]) *The Disorder of Women. Democracy, Feminism and Political Theory.* Cambridge: Polity Press.

Ricciardi, M. (2010) *La società come ordine. Storia e teoria politica dei concetti sociali.* Macerata: EUM.

Riley, P. (1982) *Will and Political Legitimacy. A Critical Exposition of Social Contract Theory in Hobbes, Locke, Rousseau, Kant and Hegel.* Harvard: Harvard University Press.

Rossdale, C. (2015) Dancing Ourselves to Death: The Subject of Emma Goldman's Nietzschean Anarchism. *Globalizations* 1: 116–133.

Rousseau, J.-J. (1992 [1750]) *Discourse on Sciences and Arts.* Masters R.D., Bush J. and Kelly C. (eds). Chicago: Dartmouth University Press.

Sapiro, V. (1992) *Vindication of Political Virtue. The Political Theory of Mary Wollstonecraft.* Chicago: The University of Chicago Press.

Schiera, P. (1986) *Il laboratorio borghese. Scienza e politica nella Germania dell'Otto-cento.* Bologna: Il Mulino.

Sklar, K.K. (2000) Introduction: "Our Rights as Moral Beings". In: Sklar K.K. (ed) *Women's Rights Emerges within the Antislavery Movement. 1830–1870. A Brief History with Documents.* Boston: Palgrave MacMillan, 1–75.

Smith, A. (2002 [1759]) *The Theory of Moral Sentiments.* Cambridge: Cambridge University Press.

Stoehr, T. (1977) *Free Love in America: A Documentary History.* New York: AMS Press.

Stokes, M. and Conway, A. (1996) (eds) *The Market Revolution in America. Social, Political and Religious Expressions, 1800–1880.* Charlottesville: University Press of Virginia.

Tocqueville, A. (2002 [1835–1840]) *Democracy in America*. Mansfield H.C. and Winthrop D. (eds). Chicago – London: The University of Chicago Press.

Todd, J. (2000) *Mary Wollstonecraft. A Revolutionary Life*. New York: Columbia University Press.

Truth, S. (1992 [1851]) "Ain't I a Woman?". In: *The Journal of American History* 81/2: 461–492.

Viola, P. (1989) *Il trono vuoto. La transizione della sovranità nella Francia rivoluzionaria*. Torino: Einaudi.

Walters, R.G. (1973) The Erotic South: Civilization and Sexuality in American Abolitionism. *American Quarterly* 2: 177–201.

Weber, M. (2001 [1905]) *The Protestant Ethic and the Spirit of Capitalism*. London: Routledge.

Wheeling, J. (2007) Anarchy in Interpretation: The Life of Emma Goldman. In: Weiss P.A. and Kensinger L. (eds) *Feminist Interpretations of Emma Goldman*. University Park: The Pennsylvania State University Press, 20–37.

Wexler, A. (2007) Emma Goldman on Mary Wollstonecraft. In: Weiss P.A. and Kensinger L. (eds) *Feminist Interpretations of Emma Goldman*. University Park: The Pennsylvania State University Press, 228–240.

Wilcox, K.R. (2009) Vindicating Paradoxes: Mary Wollstonecraft's "Woman". *Studies in Romanticism*, 3: 447–467.

Winslow, B. (1996) *Sylvia Pankhurst: Sexual Politics and Political Activism*. London: UCL Press.

Wollstonecraft, M. (2008 [1790]) A Vindication of the Rights of Men. In: Todd J. (ed) *A Vindication of the Rights of Woman and A Vindication of the Rights of Men*. Oxford: Oxford University Press.

Wollstonecraft, M. (2011 [1794]) *An Historical and Moral View of the Origin and Progress of the French Revolution*. Indianapolis: Liberty Fund.

Wollstonecraft, M. (2014 [1792]) *A Vindication of the Rights of Woman*. New Haven – London: Yale University Press.

Zerilli, L.M.G. (1994) *Signifying Woman. Culture and Chaos in Rousseau, Burke and Mill*. Ithaca – London: Cornell University Press.

CHAPTER 3

A Global Part

1 Death of a Universal

In their 1970 founding *Manifesto*, the women of the Italian collective Rivolta femminile [Female revolt] declared: "By not recognizing herself in male culture woman deprives it of the illusion of universality" (Rivolta femminile, 2018 [1970]: 228). The statement closes a document opened by the free rewriting of Olympe de Gouges' words, who almost two centuries earlier had called for a unity of women yet to be realized: "will women always be divided from one another? Will they never be a single body?" (Rivolta femminile, 1970: 227).[1] This reference to the origins of modern feminism is not intended to mark continuity; on the contrary, it highlights a distance from the foremothers who, in claiming equality with men, had only "reacted" to their exclusion from the enjoyment of rights, but had not "acted" by affirming their own radical difference (Lonzi, 1996 [1970]: 276). Treating the modern universal as an illusion, the women of Rivolta judged civil and political equality as an updated form of masculine domination. Carla Lonzi – one of the main driving forces of the collective, and certainly the most known – makes this clear with unequivocal words: "equality is what is offered to the victims of colonization on the level of laws and rights" (Lonzi, 1996 [1970]: 277).

Significantly, this departure from the discourse of rights occurs at a time when the achievements of emancipationist feminism, inaugurated by the *Declaration of the Rights of Woman and the Female Citizen*, are being consolidated and extended. The two World Wars, Nazism, Fascism, authoritarian regimes and the resistance, the rise and rejection of the Soviet regime and the workers' struggles, the first anti-colonial struggles and those for the civil rights of Black people, and the long '68 were the scene of an uninterrupted mobilization of women. The suffragist cause intertwined with the national cause, the pacifist cause or the cause for independence from colonial domination, the growing presence of women in the labor market and their rejection in the private sphere after the war, the strikes and tensions within the labor movement caused by the presence and demands of women, as well as the never

---

1 It is noteworthy that any reference to society is erased from Olympe de Gouges' quotation, which sounds as follow: "women will always have to remain isolated from each other and never make a body with society?" See de Gouges, 1792: 11–13.

sufficiently recognized but decisive role of black women in the fight against racism and segregation. All of this does not mark a linear progress, but a continuous clash – resounding or subterranean – that cuts through global history.[2] In different ways, in every part of the world, women have enlarged the space of citizenship. At the end of the '60s, however, this process manifested its limits and the claim to equality proved insufficient to express a real instance of liberation.

On July 7, 1969, the U.S. collective Redstockings – founded by Shulamith Firestone and Ellen Willis – published a seven-point *Manifesto*, which defines women as "an oppressed class" and this oppression as "total", because it affects every aspect of life. Women are exploited "as sex objects, breeders, domestic servants, and cheap labor" and the agent of oppression is man, "*all* men" (Redstockings, 2018 [1969]: 219–220). Their supremacy "is the oldest, most basic form of domination" from which all others spring – racism, capitalism, and imperialism – and which pervades "all political, economic and cultural institution". For this reason, the "final liberation from male supremacy" cannot proceed from existing institutions and ideologies (Redstockings, 2018 [1969]: 219).[3] Adopting the lexicon of class struggle, Redstockings makes women the part in charge of eradicating all forms of domination, starting with its patriarchal roots. Women are the subject of a liberation that is as total as their oppression. This partiality, now made explicit in all its global scope, allows us to shed light on the dynamics of the reproduction of domination in the processes of democratic integration. In this historical passage, the concept of woman explicitly becomes the criterion of the political[4] and is charged with a polemical content that triggers and accelerates the contemporary crisis of both citizenship and the legitimation of the modern state.

The *Redstockings Manifesto* arrived in Italy in the same year of its diffusion in the United States, and it influenced the position of Rivolta femminile. The collective arose from a specific separatist moment, namely from the polemics against the organizations of the so-called "Marxist-Leninist" left, which they viewed as incapable of recognizing the political centrality of women's struggle

---

2 Concerning all these historical events, which cannot be discussed extensively here, cf. Atwater, 1996; Locher-Scholten, 2000; Ramirez, Soysal and Shanahan, 1997; Southard, 1993; Thébaud, 1992.

3 On Redstockings and radical feminism in North America see Echols, 1989.

4 The conception of the relationship between men and women as a form of enmity could have been influenced by Valerie Solanas' SCUM *Manifesto*, which can be compared to Lonzi's work also for its criticism "of Great Art and Culture" (Ardilli, 2018: 43). Concerning Lonzi and art criticism, see Iammurri, 2016 and Zapperi, 2017.

for liberation and as guilty of reproducing dynamics of sexual oppression within themselves. The separatist gesture therefore inaugurates the *Manifesto di Rivolta femminile* and is expressed in a peremptory declaration: "woman must not be defined in relation to man" (Rivolta femminile, 2018 [1970]: 227).[5] The patriarchal signification of the concept of woman is considered the epitome of a relationship of domination that unfolds in history and in every aspect of culture. For this reason, a cut must be made. Only from a declaration of radical autonomy is it possible to affirm a "point of truth", transforming the "previous experience of women" (Lonzi, 1977 [1971]: 92), an experience of defeat and oppression, into the starting point of a "global devaluation of the world of men" (Lonzi, 1996 [1970]: 276).

Carla Lonzi puts this Nietzschean transvaluation of all values into action by engaging in a direct confrontation with Hegel, the most astute of all the "systematic thinkers" because he dressed the woman's body with an ethical meaning fundamental for the movement of the Spirit (Rivolta femminile, 2018 [1970]: 229). According to Hegel, the distinction between a "divine feminine principle and a human male principle" (Lonzi, 1996 [1970]: 279) – which assigns to the woman the task of caring for her children in the domestic space, and to the man the task of coming out of it in order to realize himself in the universal space of citizenship – is necessary in order to pass from the ethical immediacy of the ancient community to the self-conscious ethicality of the modern state (Hegel 1977 [1807]: 111 ff, 267 ff). This "phenomenology of patriarchal spirit" (Lonzi, 1996 [1970]: 281) first of all denies the "human" and therefore historical character of the subordination of woman, because it links her ethical function to her procreative capacity, such that for Hegel "the conflict of woman versus man is not perceived as a dilemma", but as a natural fact (Lonzi, 1996 [1970]: 278). Secondly, the phenomenology of patriarchal spirit identifies woman with her body, condemning her to "immanence" and thus preventing her from accessing the "stage of subjectivity" (Lonzi, 1996 [1970]: 279). Between the sexes, there is no struggle for recognition. As a consequence, woman's movement towards transcendence, which consists in becoming aware of one's own freedom by challenging the fear of death and going beyond one's immediate physical determination, is not triggered. The claim that "woman must not be defined in relation to man" means, therefore, the refusal to correspond to "a signifier in someone else's hypothesis" in order to come into the world as an "unexpected Subject" (Lonzi, 1996 [1970]: 281, 295), who is such precisely because her speech is not contemplated by the "monologue of patriarchal

---

5   Cf. Ellena, 2011: 124; on separatism, see Guerra, 2005: 25–67.

civilization" (Rivolta femminile, 2018 [1970]: 228). At the moment in which she claims "a different kind of transcendence" (Lonzi, 1996 [1970]: 295), which takes shape not through struggle but by subtraction, Lonzi exposes patriarchal history to the dissent it has hidden by treating the subordination of women as a natural fact. The emergence of the unexpected subject establishes the privileged perspective from which to make visible masculine domination in every manifestation of the culture that works ideologically to conceal it. Thus, to *Spit on Hegel* is to challenge the function of legitimation played by knowledge in relation to existing relations of domination and the dynamics of their reproduction.[6]

The integration of women into citizenship is a manifestation of these dynamics. For Lonzi, it constitutes a form of colonization because like Franz Fanon, from whom she probably draws her inspiration, she considers juridical recognition as nothing more than a concession made by the dominant to the dominated that does not involve, on the part of the latter, an autonomous affirmation of their own values against the values of those who exercise domination. In short, man remains the measure of equality, and therefore, according to Lonzi, equality consists of the recognition of women's ability to "participate in the exercise of power in society" (Lonzi, 1996 [1970]: 276). Law plays an essential function in the perpetuation of domination, which is always its hidden premise. In this case, too, it is an ideological function, since it makes the positions of its subjects mutually indifferent by homologating them into a single measure – that of the existing power relations – and conceals the power that produces differences as hierarchies within society.

The stance taken by Lonzi and the women of Rivolta in the battle over abortion – which in Italy began to be fought at the turn of the 1960s and 1970s and which only in 1978 led to the approval of the law legalizing it – is an exemplary moment in their feminist critique of the ideological effects of the law. This critique is based on a mass practice, that is, on the millions of illegal abortions that "constitute a sufficient number to consider the anti-abortion law effectively abolished" (Rivolta femminile, 1977 [1971]: 67). If this law criminalized abortion, making it a woman's fault, its legalization would have the effect of postponing the moment of awareness, when the woman would finally ask herself whether an unwanted pregnancy is due to her nature, or to man's domination over her. The feminist answer to this question is that abortion has nothing to do with the nature of the woman, that is, with her procreative capacity, but is the result of male culture that imposes "the sexuality of patriarchal man as natural

---

6   Cf. Rudan, 2020a.

sexuality for both, man and woman" (Rivolta femminile, 1977 [1971]: 68).[7] Only the pleasure of the former, in fact, involves penetration and is therefore linked to procreation, while female sexuality has a center of pleasure, the clitoris, which is autonomous from the procreative functions. The woman, therefore, becomes pregnant "at the moment when the act is performed that makes her sexually colonized" (Rivolta femminile, 1977 [1971]: 70). By sanctioning women's freedom to abort, the law would have had the effect of fixing, by way of codifying, the relationship of domination that establishes what is natural and what is unnatural on the level of sexuality, thereby making the termination of pregnancy an exclusive problem of the woman – since she is the one who "owns the uterus" (Rivolta femminile, 1977 [1971]: 70) – and consequently hiding the asymmetry of power that determined her insemination.

"Abortion is not a solution for the free woman, but for the woman colonized by the patriarchal system" (Rivolta femminile, 1977 [1971]: 73), and for this reason its legalization would only neutralize the liberating potential of the mass practice of illegal abortion:

> We will get freedom of abortion, not a new legislation on it, alongside those billions of women who make up the history of female revolt, because only then will we make this fundamental chapter of our oppression the first chapter of consciousness raising from which to undermine the structure of masculine domination.
>
> RIVOLTA FEMMINILE, 1977 [1971]: 67

The distinction between freedom and legislation is not inscribed within the classic liberal opposition between individual rights and political power. Rather, it treats the codification of rights as a mode of the reproduction of power relations. Freedom itself is not conceived as an individual right, but rather as a collective practice whose full realization requires the conscious overthrow of the fundamental conditions of existence and the continuity in time of masculine domination. Sexual politics – which, as Kate Millet observes, reconfigures the concept of woman by looking for politics in every power relationship, rather than in "that relatively narrow and exclusive world of meetings, chairmen and parties" (Millet, 2016 [1969]: 23) – is therefore charged with an explicit subversive meaning, by contesting the distinction between public and private

---

7   On the different stances in the battle for abortion in Italy, cf. Libreria delle donne di Milano, 1987: ch. 2.

and the depoliticization of the latter on which modern citizenship and the discourse of rights are based.

In Lonzi's reflection, the politics of sex takes shape through the contrast between two figures, the clitoral woman, and the vaginal woman, which do not just describe two different sexual practices, but two "responses to the masculine sexual condition and culture" (Lonzi, [1977] 1971: 84). They are presented as two extreme points – ideal types, one might say, borrowing from Weber's lexicon – between which there lies infinite objective and subjective circumstances. Lonzi, however, is not interested in these circumstances. Her goal is to bring to light a potential that exists but has not yet been deployed, the "temperamental reaction that has in itself the premises of self-consciousness" and that can therefore be considered the springboard from which to make a "leap of civilization" (Lonzi, 1977 [1971]: 91, 80). While the vaginal woman is an agent of patriarchy, who refuses autonomy from man and "guards the ideology of patriarchal virility", the clitoral woman reacts in front of the patriarch with "apocalyptic indignation" and "astonished amazement" (Lonzi, 1977 [1971]: 110, 91). She does not "tremble in every fiber of [her] being" like the servant in the Hegelian struggle for recognition (Hegel 1976 [1807]: 117), but simply repudiates the patriarch as her lord. Although she is not free from the myth of man – for no woman is in masculine civilization – she has "experienced", without any ideological trappings, "all sorts of deviations from the norm" (Lonzi, 1977 [1971]: 114) and has escaped, albeit unconsciously, from the culture of oppression which operates in the coitus.

To make room for this potential and bring it to consciousness, it is necessary to make an "act of disbelief towards the psychoanalytic dogma" (Lonzi, 1996 [1970]: 287), which has legitimized a sexuality subservient to man's pleasure and the consequent enslavement of woman (Lonzi, 1977 [1971]: 101–102). Under attack here, first of all, is Sigmund Freud, because he considered clitoral eroticism as an "immature" form of female sexuality, destined to be realized in the vaginal stage (Lonzi, 1977 [1971]: 83). Also coming under fire is Wilhelm Reich, a central reference in the 1968 anti-authoritarian mobilization and generational revolt. According to Lonzi and the women of Rivolta, his "ideology of repression" (Rivolta femminile, 1977 [1971]: 71) and the idea of the orgasm as a discharge of cosmic energy express the ignorance "of the real crisis between a colonizing sex and a colonized sex" (Lonzi, 1977 [1971]: 106). This ignorance is manifested in the myth of the complementarity between the sexes, whence derives a devaluation of clitoral sexuality as a "neurosis" which reaffirms the subjugation of woman to masculine culture (Lonzi, 1977 [1971]: 138). The road to liberation does not pass through the practice of individual sexual freedom against repression: like the woman entitled to rights, the sexually emancipated woman is only a participant of masculine culture and does not become conscious of her autonomy. To affirm this autonomy, it is necessary to recognize in the clitoris the "natural" center of the female orgasm, which frees not only pleasure from the male imperative of procreation but also the psyche of every woman from adherence to the subordinate position assigned to her by man. In this way, the game of mirrors by virtue of which she continually confirms the man in his mythological phallic virility is interrupted (Lonzi, 1977 [1971]: 86, 89–90). In Lonzi's perspective, the clitoral woman and the vaginal woman express the fracture that crosses the existing order and allows for taking a stand that prevents that order from closing and being reproduced in an undisturbed way. The concept of woman, in which imperatives of order and possibilities of revolt are stratified, becomes the signifier of this fracture, and indicates a front of deployment, invoking an active, conscious taking of sides.

This stance starts from women but does not only concern women. Abandoning the use of the term "universal", Lonzi speaks of a "global devaluation of the world of men". She considers the critique of equality as "the conclusion reached by those who, being different, intend to enact a global change in the civilization that has imprisoned them", and also recognizes in the generational rebellion a "global no … without alternatives" to the patriarchal order (Lonzi, 1996 [1970]: 276, 277, 282). The attribute "global" does not have a spatial meaning, insofar as Lonzi uses the term "planetary" to describe the dimension of the feminist movement, expressly opposing it to the "international" one practiced by the Marxist-Leninist left with which she polemicizes (Lonzi, 1996 [1970]: 288). Instead, "global" indicates the totality of relationships within which the position of the woman is as specific and partial as it is constitutional, and therefore charged with a potential for overall transformation. Masculine domination is the pillar on which the entire civilization is built, including not only sexual relations, the ideologies that legitimize them, and the institutions that formalize them – the family and marriage – but also war, imperialism, the division of the world into two opposing blocs in the context of the Cold War, and finally capitalism, both private and state:

> Historical materialism has been blind to this emotional aspect that is the key that determined the passage to private property. But that is where we must return to rediscover the archetype of property itself, the first object conceived by man: the sexual object.
>
> LONZI, 1996 [1970]: 278

Property is not – as Marxist-Leninist ideology believes – a social relationship that imposes a different access to enjoyment for individuals, but the product of the primordial acquisitive instinct of man, which he asserts by imposing his own monopoly of sexual desire. If the unconscious of man – the "absolute" subject of history and the only "tragic protagonist" of all its horrors (Lonzi, 1977 [1971]: 106), the nihilist who reckons with and dispenses death – is structured on the reduction of woman to a sexual object, the fact that she expresses an autonomous sexuality unlocks "the primal knots of the pathology of posses-siveness" (Lonzi, 1996 [1970]: 278). By asserting her desire, the woman "unveils the archetype of subjugation that is coitus as the first act of violence and hier-archical disparity between the sexes" (Lonzi, 1977 [1971]: 123). Her rebellion, however, does not aspire to the seizure of power – according to the logic of the struggle between the lord and the bondsman, which for Lonzi is also the logic of class struggle[8] – but to a liberation from power that finally opens the way to "a human relationship with all its contingencies" (Lonzi, 1977 [1971]: 87). The liberation of women does not eliminate men and therefore does not consist in an *a priori* rejection of heterosexuality: even if the latter is undeniably a pillar of patriarchy, it is up to each woman to ask herself "how much she likes or dislikes the patriarch and how much she likes or dislikes the man" (Lonzi, 1977 [1971]: 83). The problem is always the relationship with power, its recognition or delegitimization, and therefore the subjective transformation necessary to operate the coveted "global devaluation" of masculine civilization.

To affirm that woman is not to be defined by man and that the difference between man and woman is "the fundamental difference of humankind" (Lonzi, 1996 [1970]: 277) is to challenge the patriarchal production of woman and the subduing of her difference under masculine domination, thus creating the conditions for any difference to be expressed on a plane of freedom, crea-tivity and reciprocity, rather than subjugation. This rebellion would eventually subtract motherhood from the function that Hegel still assigns to it, to make it not only a free individual choice, but the physical experience of a return of consciousness to the "origins of life", an "emotional symbiosis" with the child through which the woman "dis-acculturates" herself (Lonzi, 1996 [1970]: 289), taking leave of the deadly values of masculine civilization: "we will not give our children to anyone, neither to man nor to the State. We will give them to them-selves, and we will give ourselves back to ourselves" (Lonzi, 1996 [1970]: 291).

The clitoral woman indicates a possibility of active rejection of domina-tion, an individual practice that it is up to feminism to make collective. The acknowledged centrality of sexuality as a privileged field of female revolt, how-ever, has the more or less inadvertent effect of rehabilitating the normative

---

8   On Lonzi's questionable reading of Marx, cf. Rudan, 2019.

force of the appeal to nature that Lonzi disavows with her critique of Hegel. In her discourse, nature has a double status. It is primarily the product of masculine culture, since it is man who determines what sexuality is natural in terms of his own pleasure and the reproduction of his role as an absolute subject. Nature, however, is simultaneously identified with an anatomical part, the clitoris, which allows for the assertion of an autonomous principle of pleasure. Similar to Anne Koedt, from whose *Myth of the Vaginal Orgasm* she takes inspiration (Koedt, 1969), Lonzi tries to give political value to the new scientific developments of her time and in particular to the studies of William Masters and Virginia Johnson, who had demonstrated that the nerve endings that preside over the female orgasm reside in the clitoris (Masters and Johnson, 1966). From here, it becomes possible to denounce those who, like Freud and Reich, ignored the evidence of a physiological fact – a "discovery" made by every girl through the practice of autoeroticism, well before science – to justify the greatest form of "cultural violence" ever practiced, the denial and devaluation of the clitoris as a center of pleasure (Lonzi, 1977 [1971]: 99, 78).

As a physiological insurance of a sexuality released from penetration and procreation, the clitoris can become the symbol of a specific feminine anthropological difference, of a fundamental extraneousness to domination: "what guarantees woman's lack of biological aggressiveness is her lack of penis" that makes her "a different species from the man" (Lonzi, 1977 [1971]: 131). The latter, for his part, and despite the above mentioned possibility of distinguishing between the man and the patriarch, seems condemned to remain stuck in the identity "penis-power" (Lonzi, 1977 [1971]: 111), in the archetypal structure of his unconscious that – according to Jungian theory which Lonzi draws on (Jung 1981 [1934–1954]) – is a "meta-historical invariant", which has existed since the most ancient times, such that masculine domination through sex "is an absurdity" that the women of Rivolta can hardly "consider historical" (Lonzi, 1971: 130).

The opposition between nature and culture thus ends up proposing a natural conception – no longer social or historical – of nature itself, and this is perhaps the point of greatest distance between Carla Lonzi and Simone de Beauvoir, from whom the former is inevitably inspired, even though she distances herself from the unacceptable passion for equality of the latter. In explicit continuity with Marx, Beauvoir considers nature a human and therefore historical fact. Despite the most widespread interpretations of her work, there is no distinction in her reflection between "sex" and "gender", between biology and its cultural interpretation, because the body is always a historical phenomenon that draws meaning within the social relations in which it lives and operates, as a medium of the relationship between the subject and the world and between the subject and others, as part of a "situation" objectively experienced and subjectively re-evaluated in the light of an existential project (Beauvoir, 1949: 14, 687).[9] With her critique of Hegel, Lonzi retraces Beauvoir's steps and radicalizes them by recognizing an act of domination in the ethical investment in the procreative capacity of women. For this reason, the emergence of the unexpected subject embodies a political difference and becomes the evidence of a dissent within history and the possibility of a global subversion of all domination. However, when she claims to define herself autonomously by hinging her difference on anatomy, Lonzi's woman ends up finding herself outside of history and stuck in the Hegelian sexual division of ethical labor.

The recourse to the biological fact in order to sanction an anthropological difference is what, ten years later, Monique Wittig would have effectively defined a "naturalization of history" (Wittig, 1992 [1980–1989]: 11). Like Lonzi's feminism, Wittig's "materialist lesbianism" (Wittig, 1992 [1980–1989]: 13) stems from a contestation of the dialectic. Dialectic is responsible for positing the opposition between men and women as a natural fact and of obscuring the relationship of domination that literally identifies woman with sex, and thus constitutes her as different, while man – the one who dominates ideologically, economically, and symbolically – posits himself as "universal". "Woman", therefore, would be nothing more than an "imaginary formation" (Wittig, 1992 [1980–1989]: 59) – "a myth" as Wittig says, picking up on Beauvoir – that reinterprets physical characteristics, in themselves neutral, through the network of relationships in which they are "perceived" (Wittig, 1992 [1980–1989]: 10, 12). The "production" of the woman occurs in the relationship with a man – through oppression – so that the "category of sex" that designates her and that "founds society as heterosexual" is not about her "being", but always a relationship of domination (Wittig, 1992 [1980–1989]: 11, 5–6).[10]

Language reflects this material reality, reproducing it through the categories of "woman" and "man", and thus prevents women, lesbians, and homosexuals from voicing their experience except in the terms imposed by heterosexual society. The statement "the lesbian is not a woman" can be understood from these premises: the lesbian does not indicate only a form of sexuality – a withdrawal from the "obligation of coitus" and therefore from the relationship with the man (a withdrawal which as such brings her closer to the nun) – but more broadly a practice of language, the refusal to reproduce the "straight mind" by resorting to its categories (Wittig, 1992 [1980–1989]: 20, 28). Like the clitoral

---

9   On the distinction between sex and gender in Simone de Beauvoir see at least Butler, 1986 and Moi, 2008 [1999].

10   Cf. Garbagnoli, 2013.

woman, the lesbian is thus a non-dialectical figure, the figure of an "escape" (Wittig, 1992 [1980–1989]: 13). She escapes from the "class of women" in order not to be dominated, not to submit to the oppression that pretends to determine her in a "totalitarian" way by shaping her body and her mind (Wittig, 1992 [1980–1989]: 47, 8). Unlike Lonzi, however, Wittig does not think of dialectics in terms of subjugation, of reducing sexual difference to a function of masculine domination and its reproduction. Rather, for her the dialectic is a "thought of differences" (Wittig, 1992 [1980–1989]: 43), the constant position of heterosexuality as a natural rather than a cultural and therefore historical fact. This thinking should be overcome by a "destruction" (Wittig, 1992 [1980–1989]: 81) of the categories of sex that allows for the affirmation of a new universalism that is finally indifferent to sexual determination: lesbian "represents historically and paradoxically the most human point of view", through which it is possible to challenge the existing social order and prepare for "the advent of individual subjects" that are not linguistically and therefore socially "programmed" by the heterosexual thought (Wittig, 1992 [1980–1989]: 46, 20, 10). In this way, however, the lesbian ends up finding herself out of history, placed in a dimension that is no longer archetypal but "utopian", while the concept of woman becomes exclusively the signifier of a condition of "slavery" and is removed from any possible horizon of transformation (Wittig, 1992 [1980–1989]: 35).[11] What is inevitably lost is the political character that the concept gains when it is polemically re-determined by women against masculine domination, as well as its ability to show – starting from a partiality which cannot be reduced to the pluralistic particularism of the many possible forms of sexuality – the crisis of a universal that is not simply conceived as a philosophical abstraction (Wittig, 1992 [1980–1989]: 56), but as an institutional form of the reproduction of patriarchal society through integration into citizenship.

Whatever itinerary leads to this result, to place woman outside of history is also to ignore, in a more or less deliberate way, the infinite circumstances that mark women's lives and determine their specific experience of sexual difference not only in terms of a different relationship to sexuality, but by exposing them to different intensities of oppression and exploitation in society. Like the Redstockings collective – which had repudiated "all economic, racial, educational or status privileges" (Redstockings, 2018 [1969]: 220) that divide women, so also does Lonzi declare that "the black woman is equal to the white woman" (Lonzi, 1996 [1970]: 277), going so far as to assert that the

---

11   Butler criticizes Wittig precisely because she conceives of the lesbian as a prelinguistic, presocial universal. Cf. Butler, 2010 [1990]: 31–32.

imposition of masculine sexuality is "a cultural violence unmatched by any other kind of colonization" (Lonzi, 1977 [1971]: 78). Evidently, she does not give too much weight to the physical, material, and anything but cultural violence that colonial rule had imposed on women throughout history. In a different way, but with similar outcomes, Wittig thinks of race, like woman, as an "imaginary formation" that transforms a physical characteristic in itself indifferent into a form of oppression, and thus as an effect of heterosexual thought that reproduces itself through the production of difference "in all its forms" (Wittig, 1992 [1980–1989]: 56). The purpose of materialistic lesbianism is to historicize oppression by challenging any attempt to justify it through recourse to nature, and this means, in the case of racism, treating it as the historical product of slavery (Wittig, 1992 [1980–1989]: 11). However, by making heterosexual thought the matrix of every relationship of super- and subordination, it ends up rendering indifferent the historical and therefore social determination of masculine domination, and the way in which racism also profoundly affects the possibilities of women's escape and subtraction from the heterosexual "political regime" (Wittig, 1992 [1980–1989]: 13).[12]

Slavery returns to be nothing more than a metaphor rather than a social condition, so much so that the appropriation of women as a group by the class of men is defined as "sexage", a term that echoes the French *esclavage* (Wittig, 1992 [1980–1989]: 15). The same indifference towards the social transforms the appeal to unity that the collective Rivolta entrusts to the words of Olympe de Gouges in a principle of identity unable to give an account of the condition of the workers committed to fighting against exploitation, of the proletarian housewives who in the industrial districts of Northern Italy organized themselves to claim a wage against domestic work, of the poor women for whom a clandestine abortion could mean death, or of the blacks who in the United States suffered the state policies of sterilization on racial basis.[13] In the following years, starting from these experiences and circumstances, feminism politicizes the concept of woman by starting from its social determination, making it the partial perspective through which to read and challenge not only the limits of democratic citizenship and emancipation, without any regret for the

---

12   In some recent interpretations, this reading ends up overlapping the fact of being part of a "sexual minority" with social and class subordination. See Zappino, 2019.

13   On the position of Lotta Femminista, one of the Italian groups involved in the wage for housework campaign, and on workerist feminism, see Dalla Costa, 1974 [1972]; Picchio and Pincelli, 2019; Weeks, 2011; on racist birth control policies in the US, see Davis, 1983 [1981]: ch. 12.

universal whose death Lonzi unequivocally sanctioned, but also the neoliberal transformations of society and an order of capital that had become global.

2   On the Margin

In 1977, the Combahee River Collective published a *Statement* declaring the commitment to combat "racial, sexual, heterosexual, and class oppression" by the Black lesbian and heterosexual women who comprised it. This commitment is presented as an "identity politics", which is "the most radical" in that it flows from opposition to the multiple axes of domination that are woven into the everyday experience of Black women. According to the collective, a feminist politics based only on the struggle against patriarchy could not account for this complex experience and would end up obscuring the differences that fundamentally re-determine the social effects of masculine domination (Combahee River Collective, 2017 [1977]: 17).[14] The unity and compactness given by Redstockings' radical feminism to the concept of woman is deeply questioned, while the impossibility of understanding it except from the unresolved tensions that establish its political centrality is declared.

What is expressed in the Combahee River Collective statement are movements that had subjected the Keynesian compromise to violent tension. Neoliberalism responded to these movements with transformations of welfare and the labor market that would have primarily affected the position of women, and in particular black women, in society. In this phase, neoconservatism imposed itself in the United States as a politics of the social by insisting on the need to safeguard the hold of the patriarchal family as the foundation of market freedom and a private shock absorber of the risks of individual enterprise. In the process of transformation of capitalist society, the black woman becomes a central figure in the ideological battle fought to legitimize the final coda of New Deal democracy and Johnsonian Great Society.

Neoconservatives considered the black woman as one of the main recipients of public subsidies, and the figure *par excellence* of a parasitism that calls for a radical transformation in the administration of social welfare. First ascribed to an indolent "aristocracy of welfare", then elevated to the rank of "welfare queen", she threatens both the behavioral regime imposed by the Protestant ethic, with its discipline of labor and desire, and the legitimate roles

---

14   The formula "identity politics" is used in this statement for the first time (Taylor, 2017). Cf. also Harris, 2001.

of the patriarchal family, the core of reproduction of the positions of authority responsible for giving order to the freedom of the market.[15] Only in this
framework of violent struggle for the reaffirmation of the social legitimacy of
black women is it possible to understand the repetition of Sojourner Truth's
question, *Ain't I a Woman?*, by the African American feminist bell hooks.[16] This
time the question is not asked to the white man, but to the feminist movement, which with few exceptions in history – such as the Grimké sisters or
Anna Julia Cooper (hooks, 1982: 166, 28) – had separated the question of sex
from the question of race by denying the black woman the opportunity to fight
against her own different sexual oppression. "Examining both the politics of
racism and sexism from a feminist perspective" becomes a fundamental political commitment not only for giving voice to the unexpressed experience of
the Black woman, but also for understanding the relationship between that
experience and "society as a whole" (hooks, 1982: 13). The margin occupied by
the black woman is not the condition determined by a set of factors of subjection that constitute an identity, but a perspective point that transforms that
partial condition into a potential political articulation of differences. Precisely
because of the historical and theoretical-political significance that must be
accorded to that margin, feminist theory as a political critique of society must
therefore be rethought from the perspective of the black woman.

In this operation, bell hooks moves in the wake of the crisis of the modern political universal, whose death was sanctioned by radical feminism, but
she historicizes it with a reading that starts from the American "white capitalist patriarchy", which had reproduced itself by feeding on racism and sexual oppression. The claim of equality made by women – which for her finds
its highest expression in Betty Friedan's *The Feminine Mystique* (Friedan, 1970
[1963]) and the claim for equal access to work and professions – is criticized in
light of two practical observations. First, all men are not equal. Black men have
been crushed by racist violence and segregation, while for workers – black and
white – labor has not been a tool for individual emancipation and affirmation, but an experience of exploitation. Secondly, black women have always
worked, often replacing white women in domestic tasks in exchange for a wage
to enable them to pursue careers and realize themselves as "equals" (hooks,
2000 [1984]: 1–3). Without denying the positive effects of "liberal reforms" on
women's living conditions, it must be acknowledged that they express an individualistic logic that can be easily co-opted by the "ruling capitalist patriarchy"

---

15   For a historical-political account of these transformations, see Cooper, 2017: ch. 2.
16   For an overview on bell hooks' work, see Del Guadalupe Davidson and Yancy, 2009.

(hooks, 2000 [1984]: 21, 7–8). hooks therefore recognizes the homologating dynamic of the process of democratic integration that radical feminism had brought to light by making manifest the patriarchal foundation of modern citizenship. For her, however, that process must be broken down into its material determinations. To merely acknowledge that masculine domination is the principle of all other domination is not enough; rather, it must be constantly reread from its historical operationalization.

To make woman *sans phrase* the overarching signifier of a sexual oppression common to all women is to guiltily ignore that racism has fundamentally redetermined the experience of that oppression. To ignore racism is also to erase "the class structure in American society" which "the racial politics of white supremacy" has shaped (hooks, 2000 [1984]: 3). Because it fails to account for racial and class differences and the way they are operationally articulated with sexual difference, radical feminism ends up reproducing the homologizing logic and ideological function of the modern political universal, concealing the fact that women are not only victims of domination, but can also be its agents. When it becomes synonymous with "white woman", the concept of woman is co-opted by existing social relations and guarantees their continuity. In order to interrupt this continuity, it is not enough to replace generalization with metaphor, stating that "woman is the nigger of the world", because even in this case, differences end up being erased (hooks, 1982: 141–144). Instead, it is a matter of showing the "interconnection" between patriarchy and racism, the way they produce differences put to value in the society of capital (hooks, 2000 [1984]: 19–20). In this perspective, the black woman is not a metaphor, but literally lives that interconnection and for this reason her story coincides with the history of American capitalism and is the only one that, from its partiality, can account for the totality of existing social relations and allow them to be challenged. bell hooks tells this story from the middle of the seventeenth century and more precisely from the moment when laws against "amalgamation" forbade interracial sexual relations and established a strictly separate reproduction of the slave labor force (hooks, 1982: 15). These laws therefore determine a "valorization" of black women in the market as breeders and an intensification of their trafficking, which in turn coincides with a process of discipline in which, as Angela Davis had already observed, rape plays a central role (hooks, 1982: 15–16; Davis, 1972). On the slave ship, rape is used to subjugate newly captured women who are still reluctant into accepting captivity; on the plantation, it is used to domesticate them and impose on them the hard work in the fields and in the master's house, as gatherers, servants, and breeders. Rape determines the irreducible specificity of the black woman's experience during slavery, distinguishes it from that of the male slave, and makes it, if possible, more brutal. It exhibits the inevitability of the order of racist and patriarchal society, showing white women and black men the consequences of their eventual insubordination and, precisely because of this, it is a fundamental moment of affirmation and assurance of the white man's dominance. The conditions of the dominated – black men, white women, and black women – are thus placed within a hierarchy that bell hooks does not reconstruct with an archaeological attitude and the mere intention of restoring the untold and in all cases past history of the black woman. Rather, she recognizes in the "devaluation" of her womanhood a genetic moment of the present, which continues to act in society and in the "psyches of all Americans", even after the end of slavery (hooks, 1982: 52).

Rape and labor constitute the black woman as "sexual savage" and "masculine" (hooks, 1982: 53, 22). Rape is the most brutal expression of the hatred towards women characteristic of colonial Puritan society, which considered them temptresses, sinners, and embodiments of a lust of which men are not agents, but only victims. This misogynistic regime is confirmed and intensified by slavery, which constitutes a fundamental support of Victorian morality: "as American white men idealized white womanhood, they sexually assaulted and brutalized black women" (hooks, 1982: 32). White women and black women were both subjugated, but this subjugation was expressed in one case through the repression and control of sexuality, and in the other through its continued exploitation. Consequently, the construction of the black woman as "sexual savage" sanctioned the full availability of the female slave's body – always violable precisely because it was savage – and the sexual discipline of the white woman, whose body became instead the simulacrum of a purity continuously threatened by the brutal sexuality of the black male "rapist" (hooks, 1982: 67). At the same time, the work of black female slaves in the cotton harvest and therefore outside of domestic space – in which they were obliged to carry out their servile labor – violated the boundaries of the "appropriate spheres" and therefore determined their "masculinisation", whose corollary was the "emasculation" of black men, unable to protect "their women" and therefore unable to occupy the place of the patriarch (hooks, 1982: 21–22). In the game of asymmetrical mirroring that constitutes the myth of "black matriarchy" (hooks, 1982: 71), racism becomes a foundation for the reproduction of the patriarchal order, because it conveys the idea that domination over black women is a condition of the realization of black masculinity, and because the normative efficacy of the ideology of separate spheres – and the corresponding sexual division of labor – is reinforced at the very moment when black woman's work on the plantation is considered an exception.

The patriarchal and racist definition of the black woman thus establishes a specific position, one that is not assimilated to the sexual oppression of the white woman nor to the racial oppression of the black man. It acquires a societal function as part of a complex system of hierarchies of which she constitutes the basis and source of legitimacy. Reconstructing the history of that definition does not imply a cancellation of the experiences of white women and black men, but it does make it necessary to account for them within the set of social relations that produce and reproduce differences as hierarchies.

Even when it claims to be an innovative way of governing society, neoconservatism draws heavily on the representations of black sexuality that had taken shape during slavery with the intention of blaming blacks for their marginalization in order to relieve the state from the responsibility of taking care of it. In 1965 Daniel Patrick Moynihan presented a famous report, with which bell hooks was directly confronted, in which black women – "masculine" and sexually undisciplined – were indicated as the cause of a "tangle of pathology" that called into question the family, its figures of authority, and its function of "socialization" (Moynihan 1965). The intervention – which sets the tone for the entire subsequent debate – is intended to support the abolition of subsidies in favor of families with dependent children, of which blacks were the major and direct beneficiaries,[17] but for hooks it makes clear above all the function played by racist sexism to support the transformations of capitalism.

Unemployment had undermined the model of the "family wage", a form of redistribution of wealth centered on the figure of the worker-head of the family, forcing an increasing number of women to work. Within this framework, the accusation of the "black matriarchy" has the effect of imposing "upon the consciousness of the American public the notion that any career woman, any woman who competed with men, was envious of male power and was likely to be a castrating bitch" (hooks, 1982: 180). Racism thus reinforces the ideology of separate spheres in order to legitimize and compensate for the dismantling of welfare while simultaneously re-determining the form of social relations. While black men – according to a dynamic like the one described by Gloria Anzaldúa to analyze the *machismo* of Latino migrants (Anzaldúa, 1987: 83–84) – express their resentment towards castrating black women, these women blame the men who are not up to their patriarchal function (hooks, 1982: 88, 94 ff). The transformations of capitalism and its political administration exacerbate the fragmentation and forms of subordination that had already manifested themselves in the age of slavery, when black women and men had embraced

---

17   Cf. Cooper, 2017: 37 ff.

the model of the patriarchal family and the sexual division of labor as an escape route from their racist oversexualization, and when white women had in fact legitimized the rape of black women by embracing the Victorian morality that guaranteed them, thanks to the degradation of slaves, not to fall into the lowest position in the social hierarchy (hooks, 1982: 44, 47–49). The increase in cases of masculine violence against black women by black men is the outcome of this process, an exorbitant display of masculine strength necessary to affirm and ensure the cogency – more symbolic than material – of patriarchal fig-ures of authority (hooks, 1982: 103–105).[18] Just as it had been fundamental to the orderly reproduction of slave society and to the hierarchical production of the dominated and their "identity" (hooks, 1982: 19), the masculine violence fomented by the racist sexism of the social sciences – which at this historical height have a function of legitimizing relations of domination more than the philosophy against which Lonzi had lashed out – also plays an essential role at the origins and during the process of the neoliberal reorganization of society.

In this analysis, black women are central neither because of their numerical or statistical relevance, or as a separate and subordinate category experienc-ing a specific condition that must be accounted for with sociological accuracy. Rather, by breaking the myth of the black community nurtured by the neo-conservatives themselves, bell hooks brings black women to the center of the movement of capitalist society, and in this sense her analysis acquires signifi-cance outside the U.S. context as well. Capitalist society presents itself in the form of a historically determined "interconnection" between different systems of domination within which the positions of the dominated are empirically related to each other but differentiated according to different possibilities of access to social power conferred by sex, skin color, and money. For this reason, at the moment it is placed at the center of the history of capital, the concept of woman incorporates a perspective point that prevents any abstrac-tion and that simultaneously makes it necessary to think about differences from their systematic connection within the reproduction of society and its transformations.

Feminist and anti-racist political discourse is therefore obliged to con-front the way in which the "interconnections" between different systems of domination hierarchically distribute social power, establishing among those who are dominated not an immediate identity or even forms of solidarity, but relationships of superiority and subordination. Historically, however, this has not occurred. Throughout the nineteenth century, with few exceptions, the

---

18   On the issue of masculinity, see also hooks, 2004.

anti-slavery and anti-segregationist movement either underplayed or remained silent on the issue of the rape of black women so as not to raise the scandal in Puritan and Victorian society, and overshadowed the suffragist cause so as not to run the risk of damaging the struggle for black liberation. In the twentieth century, the leaders of the movement embraced a patriarchal discourse to the point that masculine domination, the seduction of white women, and the subjugation of black women became so many symbols of black power. As for feminism, it gave the hierarchical model of race and sexual relations established by white capitalist patriarchy a different shape:

> Women liberationists did not invite a wholistic analysis of woman's status in society that would take into consideration the varied aspects of our experience. In their eagerness to promote the idea of sisterhood, they ignored the complexity of woman's experience. While claiming to liberate women from biological determinism, they denied women an existence outside that determined by our sexuality.
>
> HOOKS, 1982: 190[19]

The rhetoric of sisterhood – which emerges in all its force in the famous anthology edited in 1970 by Robin Morgan, entitled *Sisterhood is Powerful* (Morgan, 1970) – replicates the biological determinism that makes sex the only significant factor in women's existence and produces among them an identity in oppression that abstracts from the historical conditions of their experience (hooks, 1982: 190). If "oppression" means "absence of choices" (hooks, 2000 [1984]: 5), we must recognize that, in the historical conditions determined by capitalism, patriarchy is organized in such a way as to differentiate the spheres and possibilities of choice for each individual woman and among women who are in socially different positions. Thus, for example, while white feminism has fought against the family by identifying it with the main institution of masculine domination, for black women the existence of a domestic space free from the threat of the white man, although not necessarily free from patriarchal relations, has meant creating the conditions to conceive and practice a distance from the violence and humiliation suffered daily in racist society, and to build relationships of solidarity without which no political revolt against racism could have taken place (hooks, 2015 [1990]: 42–48). On the other hand, far from being only oppressed, white women have also exercised the power

---

19   On the relationship between black feminism and social movements in the U.S., see Roth, 2004.

conferred to them by their skin color and money and have been in many cases – first as slave masters, then as masters of domestic servants, but also as supervisors in factories – the first and direct counterpart of black women in exploitative relationships (hooks, 2000 [1984]: 50).

By identifying the condition of all women with an exclusively sexual oppression, feminism denied the existence of power asymmetries among women and gave up criticizing capitalist society in order to protect the interests of women from privileged classes (hooks, 2000 [1984]: 102).[20] At the same time, even as it took up the anti-racist cause, this feminism neither saw nor challenged the relations of sexual domination within the black community, failing to recognize the function of a "connector" between white men and black men performed by patriarchy (hooks, 1982: 99). Like Chandra Talpade Mohanty, who since the late 1980s has criticized sisterhood from a postcolonial perspective (Mohanty, 2003: 106 ff), bell hooks does not see it as the premise of feminism, a unity naturally granted by a common oppression, but the result of a process capable of confronting, even through open hostility, with power differences among women (hooks, 1984: 43 ff.). If feminism is a struggle to end masculine domination, it must practice a discourse capable of considering not only "the personal that is political", thus recognizing each singular experience as part of a set of social relations, but also of criticizing "the politics of society as a whole, and global revolutionary politics" (hooks, 2000 [1984]: 27). Projected into this global horizon, the concept of woman cannot establish the general signifier of all oppression, but it can indicate a position that is partial in a twofold sense: one empirical, in that it is a specific part of society, and the other epistemological and political, because it allows us to shed light on the set of dynamics of its reproduction and articulate against domination the different positions that capitalism produces and reproduces as hierarchies.

In this perspective, feminism can neither be separatist – preaching and practicing relationships between women only – or be reduced to identity politics. Beginning with this conviction, bell hooks openly criticizes the Combahee River Collective's *Statement*: while declaring the need to develop "an integrated analysis and practice based on the fact that the major systems of oppression are interlocking", and by openly polemicizing with the black power movement and white feminism, the Collective had chosen to create a separate realm of discourse and initiative for black women (Combahee River Collective, 2017 [1977]: 15). Without denying the positive effects of this move – first, that of creating the conditions for the black women's feminist speaking out – bell

---

20   Cf. also hooks, 2009 [2000]: ch. 9.

hooks considers this separatist response as "reactionary" precisely because it elides the communication, confrontation, and clash necessary to offer "all women a feminist ideology uncorrupted by racism" (hooks, 1982: 151–152 and 2000 [1984]: 73). Further, when it is not reactionary, separatism is "impossible", because in capitalist society "none of us are truly separate" (hooks, 2000 [1984]: 78–79). In order to take on the complexity of women's experience, it is necessary to consider it globally, recognizing the way in which capitalism has transformed patriarchy and racism into its own operational gears by re-determining their societal function. The problem is therefore not to establish a precedence – whether symbolic or chronological – and therefore a hierarchical order of political priorities between different systems of domination, as radical feminism had done. Rather, it is to recognize once again their "interconnection", and that "one system cannot be eradicated while the others remain intact" (hooks, 2000 [1984]: 20, 37).

The Black woman is the one who embodies this possibility epistemologically as much as politically, because her position in society is established at that point in which patriarchy, racism, and exploitation act simultaneously. Since it can only be understood from the interconnection, her "marginality" can be reversed into an advantage, becoming the condition of possibility of a critical stance that allows the challenging of existing social hegemony, as well as the building of what the Jamaican sociologist Stuart Hall, taking up Antonio Gramsci, has called a "counter-hegemony". The margin, in this sense, does not define black women's complete foreignness to domination, as it was for Carla Lonzi's "unexpected Subject", because every woman wields power, as much to oppress as to resist oppression. Nor is the margin the condition "imposed by [an] oppressive structure", a merely objective condition, but the position chosen "as site of resistance, as location of radical openness and possibility" (hooks, 2015 [1990]: 22). To occupy that position means "to be part of the whole but outside the main body" and by virtue of this to formulate a "world view" distinct from that of those exercising domination, an "oppositional world view" (hooks, 2000 [1984]: xvi) that makes manifest the lines that divide and contrast the oppressed and the oppressors and simultaneously the way they are articulated in a contradictory system of socially determined hierarchies. Taking a stand on the margin means choosing which side to be on within power relations.

According to bell hooks, this stance allows for the practice of what Stuart Hall – who in the same years treated the issue of race as central, though forgotten, to the social sciences – called a politics of "articulation". This is the process of producing a discourse that connects different and distinct elements, the articulation of which, however, is not "necessary" because it is not established by any form of "belonging" (Hall and Grossberg, 1986: 53). Even if it refers to a specific "social group", the articulation does not arise from a deterministic relationship between a subject, its social or class condition, and what this subject thinks, but on the contrary, it makes the subject emerge at the moment when, by making its specific historical situation intelligible, it gives it power. In this way, discourse can "produce" a social movement that is not internally homogeneous and whose unity is neither necessary nor precedes discourse, but is the effect of its articulation (Hall and Grossberg, 1986: 50, 55).[21] The feminist politics of articulation, therefore, cannot disregard the Black woman and her condition, the commitment to listen to and recount her "broken voice" and grasp her suffering (hooks, 2015 [1990]: 146). At the same time, however, the politics of articulation allows those who, in different ways, are "at the center" to take a stand on the margin even if they do not share it as an objective condition.

The story that bell hooks tells in *Ain't I a Woman* must be reconstructed so that it is clear that a politics of liberation must necessarily impact the different systems of domination, otherwise it will be ineffective. The Black Woman, then, is not the signifier of an "identity politics" like the one proudly claimed by the Combahee River Collective or, more precisely, her identity determined by interconnection is as singular as it is global and therefore indicates the possibility of breaking down socially constituted identities by establishing a field of communication between subjects – white women, black men, workers – who are in different positions in a social totality that reproduces itself by transforming differences into hierarchies and lines of enmity among the dominated (hooks, 2015 [1990]: 145–151).

This partiality is what distinguishes the politics of the "margin" from the politics of "intersectionality". Formulated for the first time in 1989 by the African American jurist Kimberlé Crenshaw, who drew on the reflections of bell hooks, Angela Davis and, more generally, of North American black feminism, the intersectional perspective originally aimed to effectively correct discriminations that are not covered by existing judicial precedents within the common law system. Considering three trials handed down following the complaints of some black women workers, who challenged unlawful dismissals and lack of career advancement, Crenshaw shows that their cases were examined from

---

21   For Hall, the concept of articulation has a double status: the first, which draws on the reading of Marx developed by Althusser, is historico-critical and allows us to analyze the position of racism in a given "social formation", then as a component of capitalist society; the second is political and allows us to understand the mode of production of a hegemonic and counterhegemonic discourse (Hall and Grossberg, 1986: 53–55; Hall 1996 [1980]); see also (Althusser, 1969 [1965]: 175 ff; Althusser and Balibar, 2016 [1968]: 180 ff).

the precedents related to discrimination of a purely sexual or racial nature. Discrimination against black women, however, occurs "at the intersection" of sex and race, and this very fact offers a privileged perspective on the law: while she cannot be "represented" by either the white woman or the black man, the black woman can represent both (Crenshaw, 1989: 167, 143).

Practicing an intersectional administration of justice, consequently, would "facilitate the inclusion of marginal groups for whom it can be said: 'when they enter, we all enter'" (Crenshaw, 1989: 167). Crenshaw quotes the words of Anna Julia Cooper to assert a universalist perspective. Because the specificity of her condition is not recognized by law, the black woman is the figure charged with extending its reach and realizing its universality. The margin, consequently, is read as an objective condition from which to free oneself, rather than as a political perspective point, and is in this way depoliticized. Even beyond Crenshaw's intentions to "develop language which is critical of the dominant view and which provides some basis for unifying activity" (Crenshaw, 1989: 167, 149), the politics of intersectionality risks resolving itself into a catalog of conditions of oppression that are as specific – because they are produced by the intertwining of an indefinite multiplicity of factors – as they are equivalent. Reduced to legal cases, intersectional identities can always be co-opted within the identity politics introduced by the neoliberal administration of law to neutralize any form of collective claim through the individual compensation of the various conditions of social disadvantage.[22] On the contrary, insofar as it expresses the taking of a stance, a deployment oriented towards transforming the interconnections established by white capitalist patriarchy into a politics for liberation, bell hooks' margin aims to interrupt this fragmentation by making feminism a "mass-based movement" (hooks, 2000 [1984]: 29). bell hooks writes, "although the focus is on the black female, our struggle for liberation has significance only if it takes place within a feminist movement that has as its fundamental goal the liberation of all people" (hooks, 1982: 13). Placing the concept of woman on the margin allows us to articulate "interconnection" not as an identity but as a process and a movement – not as a wish for a generic alliance between oppressions, but as a political perspective on the totality of social relations. The concept of woman thus acquires the global character that determines its political centrality at a time when it is capitalist society itself that becomes global under the impetus of post-colonial movements.

---

22   On the relationship between identity, rights, and the law, see Brown, 1995. For a critical discussion of the category of intersectionality, see Brown, 2002: 420–434; Ferrari, 2013: 29–49; Moi, 2017: ch. 4.

3   The Difference

In the mid-1980s, the "co-optation" of feminism within the existing social, political, and institutional structures denounced by bell hooks becomes a legit-imizing factor in the process of globalization of capital. In 1985, the third World Conference on Women, organized in Nairobi by the United Nations, took stock of the "Decade for Women" inaugurated in 1975 in Mexico City by addressing the so-called debt crisis and the conditions of "economic disadvantage" expe-rienced by countries that after World War II had achieved independence from colonial rule. Acknowledging this disadvantage, the programmatic document approved in Nairobi renews the commitment to promote equality between men and women – where equality means "equal opportunities" to individually enhance their human resources in the marketplace – and to ensure the full integration of women in any effort of "total development", not only economic but "human". In all cases, integration must take place in accordance with "the objectives of a new international economic order" (United Nations, 1985).

The development/underdevelopment dichotomy that supports the con-stitution of this order is taken up by the human and social sciences and also runs through feminist political theory. The construction of the "Third World woman" as an object of research thus ends up legitimizing the policies of debt – from structural adjustment plans to forms of microcredit in support of small individual businesses – which contribute to shaping the process of the constitution of the global market. According to Mohanty, this is a precise colonialist "strategy" of the "suppression of heterogeneity" aimed at sustaining Western "ethnocentric universalism" (Mohanty, 2003: 18, 21) and legitimizing the order of capital. There is a continuity between the construction of "sexual difference" as the uniform subjection of women to masculine domination, on the one hand, and on the other hand that of the "Third World" as an "immobile and ahistorical" condition that burdens all women who inhabit it. Deprived of sexual freedom, ignorant, poor, bound to tradition (cultural or religious) and to domestic life by virtue of her sex and her geographical location, the "Third World woman" is the counterpart and the condition of existence of the eman-cipated Western woman – educated, modern, master of her own body and of her own choices – who in turn becomes the normative model that presides over the process of development, implicitly making the West and capitalism "the primary referent in theory and praxis" (Mohanty, 2003: 22, 270).

The heterogeneity suppressed in this operation is not the "cultural" one, but the set of historical-concrete differences that mark women's lives in the global world. Rather than placing the First and Third Worlds – and the women who inhabit them – along a progressive, already-drawn, and unquestionable line of development, from a feminist perspective the problem is to bring the "complex interconnections" (Mohanty, 2003: 20) that exist between the two worlds to light, showing how race and class globally re-determine the sexed experience. In Mohanty's perspective, the differences that polemically cut through the concept of woman allow us to articulate a critique of the universal – the modern political universal that takes Man as referent and the sociological-anthropological universal that constructs the Third World woman as the object of science – in order to affirm difference as a partiality that allows us to comprehend and contest the global order altogether: "the challenge is to see how differences allow us to explain the connections and border crossings better and more accurately, how specifying difference allows us to theorize universal concerns more fully" (Mohanty, 2003: 226).

It is also in this case a stance "on the margin" that does not consider all positions of marginality as equivalent, but recognizes the existence of a "potential epistemic privilege" (Mohanty, 2003: 235) operating within global capitalism: it is the point of view of poor and working women of the Third World – considered from the irreducible specificity of their condition – that "provides the most incisive viewing of systemic power" from which to organize scientific research and political initiative (Mohanty, 2003: 232).

Gayatri Chakravorty Spivak also recognizes in this project the "common struggle" that unites her to bell hooks and Mohanty, whose works she declares to have placed on the same shelf of her *Critique of Postcolonial Reason* (Spivak, 1999: XI).[23] What ties them together is the problem of thinking sexual difference as a political difference, as a partial perspective that is as capable of showing the fracture that constitutes the social as it is of affirming it politically within the historical coordinates that define the social as a capitalistic order. The post-colonial gaze becomes an integral part of this project and mobilizes the differences that polemically constitute the concept of woman by redefining it both from the historical point of view and thus from that of critique.

From a historical perspective, Spivak thinks of the post-colonial as the process in which the "colonial narrative" is transferred into the dynamics of financialization of the globe and justifies them as inevitable (Spivak, 1999: 3). Since the discourse of Development incorporates and reproduces, while transforming, the logic that presides over colonial domination, the feminist critique of that discourse must account for the ideological and political reorganization of globalized capital. Spivak sharply criticizes the United Nations conferences on women because in the name of woman, and through the establishment

---

23   For a general discussion of Spivak's work, see Iuliano, 2012.

of an international feminist bureaucracy (Spivak 1999: 370), they support the neoliberal "new economic order" and provide an "alibi" for the perpetuation of exploitation (Spivak, 1999: 2–3).[24] Through these conferences, the financialization of the world is legitimized by the staging of a "global national unity" between the North and the South, which in this paradoxical form serves to define "the profound transnational disunity necessary for globalization" (Spivak, 1996b: 2). While the daily struggles of women in decolonized contexts are silenced by the United Nations' careful selection process of nongovernmental organizations, the microcredit programs of which Southern women are individual beneficiaries multiply a social as well as political fragmentation that for Spivak supports the centralization of capitalist command. Women's conferences thus create the illusion of an "international civil society" (Spivak, 1996c: 249) – of a sphere in which individual and collective claims for redistribution of wealth can be activated – which obscures the reconfiguration of the role and functions of the state in the global context. In order to bring to light the differences that polemically cut through the concept of woman in the post-colonial global world, it is necessary to shed light on the strategies of social, political, and institutional fragmentation that sustain the process of capital's globalization. The feminist critique of the "post-colonial reason" that shapes that process takes its cue from the need to account for the way in which the "culture of development" – which operates concretely through the establishment of special economic zones, international procurement, and the "post-Fordist" organization of production – "reconstitutes women" (Spivak, 1996c: 257).

The premise of the feminist critique of post-colonial reason must therefore be a post-colonial critique of the concept of woman. By "post-colonial" Spivak does not mean a location in space, but a position in history, a perspective marked by the prefix post- that simultaneously indicates discontinuity with the colonial past and its operationalization in the present. The most urgent political claims advanced within decolonized countries are articulated through the conceptual constellation of the European Enlightenment – nation, constitution, citizenship, democracy, sovereignty – inherited from the colonial era. However, when they are mobilized outside the context that generated them, the gap between those concepts and their historical referent, between the signifier and the signified, is accentuated. This gap, for Spivak, is the starting point of the work of deconstruction and thus inaugurates the possibility of

---

24   The problem of the "complicity" of feminism with neoliberalism is also provocatively discussed by Nancy Fraser (2013).

a "persistent critique of what one cannot not want" (Spivak, 1993–1994: 28) by means of showing its discursive, and therefore historical, production, and placing the concepts "under erasure" – to use Jacques Derrida's terms – which means making a provisional use of them while knowing that they "no longer [operate] within the paradigm in which they were originally generated" (Spivak, 1996 [1985a]: 125; Derrida, 1967: 89). The concept of woman is itself subjected to this operation of "erasure" that indicates simultaneously the need for "taking a stand", a "declaration of interest" that presides over the critique, and the non-definitive character of the definition that moves the critique itself:

> my own definition of a woman is very simple: it rests on the word 'man' ... you might say at this point, defining the word 'woman' as resting on the word 'man' is a reactionary position. should i not carve out an independent definition for myself as a woman? ... the only way I can see myself making definitions is in a provisional and polemical one: I construct my definition ... not in the terms of a woman's putative essence, but in the terms of words currently in use. 'Man' is such a word in common usage. not a word, but the word. I therefore fix my glance upon this word even as i question the enterprise of redefining the premises of any theory.
>
> SPIVAK, 1996 [1985b]: 54

Insofar as its premise is "Man" – a "unifying concept" that makes abstraction from all concrete differences, hides them, and in this way constitutes itself as the "sovereign subject as author, the subject of authority, legitimacy, and power" (Spivak, 1996 [1985b]: 55 and 1996 [1985c]: 210) – political theory is indeed a "patriarchal monologue", as Carla Lonzi held. For Spivak, however, it is not possible to interrupt this monologue through a gesture of simple subtraction, that is, with the nominalist claim to define woman autonomously and outside of the relationship that constitutes the referent of the discourse. Woman, therefore, is presented in Spivak's critique as a concept that is both divisive – because it expresses a deliberate partiality that polemically fractures the unity represented by the concept of man – and internally divided, because it is the product of the same social relationship that it contests, as well as its historical determinations.

Reading the texts of Italian feminism of difference and Marxist feminism of the 1970s and 1980s – from Lonzi and Rivolta femminile to the Libreria delle donne in Milan, via the Lotta Femminista's documents on wage for housework – Spivak claims to have appreciated them, but registers with ill-concealed dismay that they do not account for the domestic work of migrant women from decolonized countries that supported the transformations of

Italian industry at that time, or the role played by the multinational clothing company Benetton in the "post-Fordist feminization" of labor (Spivak,
1996c: 261).[25] This observation is not intended to deny the political centrality
of the "coding of value" of the sexed body (Spivak, 2009 [1993]: 22), nor does it
simply invite sociological scrupulousness in accounting for the ways in which
race and class affect the condition of women. In order to avoid the "essentialist freezing" of concepts – such as the one Lonzi falls into when she places
women outside of history and makes their sexual determination a condition
of existential and political extraneousness to masculine domination – it is
necessary to continuously investigate their "situational production" (Spivak,
1996 [1985b]: 62). The post-colonial critique of the concept of woman therefore consists in a constant work of historicization, where by "history" Spivak
does not mean an "antiquarian" operation, or small stories intended to interrupt the line of the "great European narrative" (Spivak, 2009 [1993]: 71, 74).[26] It
is rather an exposition of facts – a *Darstellung*, in the Marxian sense, a "staging
of the world in representation" (Spivak, 1999: 264; Marx, 1996 [1867]: 19–20) –
which proceeds by recognizing the centrality of protagonists different from
those chosen according to "conventional standards" and that, precisely for
this reason, allows to establish a different "truth" than that provided by the
dominant narratives (Spivak, 1996 [1993–1994]: 26–27). Making history of the
concept of woman means, in other words, to affirm a partial perspective on
history that is the premise for a feminist critique of the global order.

In light of her wholly specific place in that order, in that her position is
defined as "between Patriarchy and Development" (Spivak, 1999: 296), the
"subaltern woman" is for Spivak the privileged and necessary referent of this
critique:

> the subaltern woman is now to a rather large extent the support of pro-
> duction. ... In the new international economic order after the dissolution
> of the Soviet Union, it is the labor of the patriarchally defined subaltern
> woman that has been most effectively socialized.
>
> SPIVAK, 1999: 67–68

---

25   Spivak documentary sources are Bono and Kemp, 1991; Cicogna and De Lauretis, 1990.
      About migrant women's domestic labor in Italy between 1960s and 1980s, and about the
      lack of interest on their condition from the feminist collectives, see Gissi, 2018: 55.
26   One can point out in this regard the proximity between Spivak and Mohanty's critique
      of *herstory*, understood as a history of women that is local and separate from the larger
      masculine and Western narrative (Mohanty, 2003: 119 ff).

The "stance" that kicks off the critical work consists in the risky operation of assigning a specific "literal referent" to the name woman, namely the one that "strictly, historically, geopolitically speaking, we cannot imagine as a literal referent" (Spivak, 1999: 331 and 2009 [1993]: 155–156), since her history and her voice have been silenced by the position of subordination she occupies in the global relations of domination and exploitation. This operation – which Spivak describes by resorting to the rhetorical figure of "catachresis" (Spivak, 2009 [1993]: 155, 182–184) – is for her the expression of a "strategic essentialism" that does not consist in the affirmation of an ontological conception of sexual difference but presupposes a "notion of the social as essence" (Spivak, 1996a: 294) that determines the content of the concept of woman. The latter, in short, incorporates a specific social determination which cannot be disregarded when the aim is that of criticizing what essentially poses itself as "the social". Therefore, the "strategy" does not consist in the production of a theory based on stable definitions, but in a mobilization of keywords that can have a critical function only starting from their deconstruction, that is, from their systematic and incessant historicization. Making the subaltern woman the referent of the concept of woman is an inverse operation with respect to that of abstraction that constructs "Man" as a unifying concept or "woman" as a unitary signifier of oppression, because it does not erase differences, but affirms an irreducible difference from which it is possible to account for the totality of social relations. Giving voice to the subaltern woman – as Spivak does by reading "into the pores" of colonial historiography, as well as Western philosophy and literature, and by bringing to the center the specific working conditions of women in the Global South along transnational value chains – means establishing a different truth capable of delegitimizing the discourse of Development that sustains the globalization of capital through the constant production of the subaltern as different.

Describing the condition of the subaltern woman in the global market, Spivak says that her labor "is most effectively socialized" but also that she "is affected remotely by socialized capital" (Spivak, 1996a: 292). The two statements are obviously contradictory, but they are both validated by the idea, taken from Marx, that it is possible to export capitalist exploitation without simultaneously exporting its mode of social production.[27] By affirming the coexistence of the formal and real subsumption of labor to capital – taking up the Marxian terms she uses – Spivak is able to show that the subaltern woman is integrated into the global order because her labor is placed under

---

27   The reference is to Marx, 1998 [1894]: 213.

the command of capital, although she lives and works in conditions of production and reproduction that the latter does not directly organize. The family is a relevant example of this peculiar condition. It is a patriarchal institution within which what takes shape is what Spivak calls – by way of a confrontation with the French feminism of Julia Kristeva, Hélène Cixous, Antoinette Fouque, and Luce Irigaray – a symbolic "effacement of the clitoris", namely the appropriation of the woman's body and her procreative capacities for the sake of the ordered transmission of the property and the name of the father (Spivak, 1987 [1981]: 151 and 1996 [1985b]: 70). The symbolic effacement of the clitoris is the expression of a patriarchal constant that moves between different epochs and modes of production, but can only be understood historically. A "class analysis of families" requires us to examine the coexistence on a global level of a capitalist model of the nuclear family, oriented towards consumption, and of an "extended" or "corporated" family (Spivak, 1996 [1985b]: 59–60), which, however, cannot be considered a sort of archaic remnant that is *outside* the capitalist order. On the contrary, it contributes to the production of women as a pool of cheap and fully available labor, which as such can be exploited in factories or in the home, always at the service of large multinational corporations (Spivak, 1996 [1985b]: 70).

The home-based piecework for the clothing industry – to which Mohanty had also devoted attention, taking up the studies of Maria Mies (Mies, 1998 [1986]) – is an example of how even domestic space is transformed into a site of production, within which women's "affective labor", considered as "naturally feminine," is exploited in order to make the workers themselves pay for the costs of their reproduction and to reduce wages (Spivak, 1996 [1985a]: 118–119).[28] Spivak's problem is not to treat the subjugation of women, the male monopoly of their sexual desire, and its institutionalization as the founding moment of the capitalist social order, but to investigate the way in which the latter reconfigures women's position and masculine domination in the historical moment in which it achieves global extension.

Giving voice to the subaltern by bringing to the forefront the social essence of the concept of woman, i.e., its global capitalist determination, allows Spivak to contest the discourse of Development. The position of women workers in the Global South cannot be read along a linear trajectory at the head of which

---

28 In *Scattered Speculations on the Question of Value* and *Feminism and Critical Theory*, Spivak discusses the issue of women's "affective labor" in order to reread Marx's theory of value. On the specificity of her position to that articulated by Marxist feminism see Rudan, 2020b. For a survey of how Marxist feminism has addressed the issue of reproductive labor, see Arruzza, 2016 and Bhattacharya, 2017.

is the financially and technologically advanced capitalism of the Global North, with its promise of emancipation from relations of domination. On the contrary, for Spivak it is necessary to make manifest the connection between radically heterogeneous conditions, while revealing what technologically advanced or "post-industrial" Western capital has hidden by displacing it in the "rest of the world": "economic coercion as *exploitation*" (Spivak, 1996 [1985a]: 124). Concretely, this means that while Lehman Brothers, thanks to computers, can make $2million in 15 minutes, "the entire economic text would not be what it is if it could not write itself as a palimpsest upon another text where a woman in Sri Lanka has to work 2,287 minutes to buy a t-shirt" (Spivak, 1996 [1985a]: 129).

The sex of the workforce in this scheme is crucial and does not simply depend on the fact that, as it is commonly said, "Oriental women have small and supple fingers" (Spivak, 1996 [1985b]: 69). Rather, at the heart of the discourse is the articulation of the relationship between patriarchy and capitalism in transnational value chains, and thus the way in which patriarchal social relations contribute to the "production [of women] as the new focus of super-exploitation" (Spivak, 1996 [1985a]: 124). If the discourse of Development makes the First World the fate of the Third and on this basis promotes financial interventions of debt imposition and dependency construction, the position of the subaltern woman requires looking beyond the "cant of modernization" to recognize "that the 'postmodern' … reproduces the 'premodern' on another scene" (Spivak, 1996 [1985a]: 126). This scene does not necessarily coincide with decolonized geographic space. Contemporary migrations, in fact, globally mobilize the post-colonial condition, since subalternity is reproduced in the metropolis and is simultaneously in constant relation with subalternity in decolonized space. More than looking for a causal link between the poverty of the Global South and the migrations towards the North, Spivak wants to bring to light their relation and simultaneous action, their interconnection, as bell hooks would say. In fact, the discourse of Development continually tends to conceal the fact that Bangladeshi migrants from East London, who work at home for the multinational textile industry, are inevitably linked to the unskilled workers who work in the textile industry implanted in Bangladesh in an export processing zone. The condition of the latter, however, is considered the positive mark of Development – of integration through labor – which transforms the connections established by capital along value chains into a form of competition that hinders the possibility of communication and collective action, for example on the trade union level (Spivak, 1999: 414, 378).

The condition of the subaltern reveals that the reproduction of capital as a global social relation is not the planetary extension of a homogeneous mode of production modeled on its most technologically advanced forms, but consists in the synchronization and connection within the logic of accumulation of heterogeneous spaces and times that are produced as such: the domestic space of "affective labor" and the space designed by transnational value chains; the time of the virtual instantaneousness of financial capital and the time of the extension and intensification of the working day; those spaces segmented by the establishment of hierarchies of citizenship and those of special economic zones that respectively organize the mobility of labor and that of capital.[29]

The experience of the subaltern from which Spivak proposes the always provisional reconfiguration of the concept of woman thus allows us to bring to light the "transnational" form of economic and political organization of global capital. The latter produces heterogeneous conditions that are systematically put to value in the process of accumulation and establishes political differentials that are as necessary to its expansion and reproduction as they are indicative of the overall transformations of the contemporary state. To describe these, Spivak uses the formula "global state" (Spivak, 1999: 276). The global state does not describe a world political-institutional order, but instead indicates the priority of executive powers over representative ones, which constitutes it as a "managerial state", and the end of the Keynesian nexus between labor and citizenship (Butler and Spivak, 2007: 79).[30] Citizenship cannot be considered "idealistically", that is, by ignoring the fact that it has been historically realized through the subordination of women, indigenous people, the indigent, homosexuals, and migrants. However, it is possible to recognize that even the figure of the "abstract individual as citizen", at whose service the state is placed, is dissolved by "transnationality". The latter undermines the arrogant "temporizing focused by the Industrial Revolution" (Spivak, 1996c: 248), that is, the idea of a process in which economic development coincides with the progressive democratic extension of citizenship rights.

In this transnational framework, precisely because it is expressed through a catachresis that makes visible the gap between the concept of woman and its literal referent, the condition of the subaltern woman – characterized by an access to work to which there does not correspond the achievement of an "infrastructural support" that can give her a social "possibility of mobility" (Spivak, 1996a: 292) – is as specific as it is indicative of a global trend. "There is no state on the globe today that is not part of the capitalist economic system or can want to eschew it fully" (Spivak, 1999: 84). This means that no state can "escape the orthodox constraints of a 'neo-liberal' world economic system"

---

29   Cf. Ricciardi, 2017: 108–124.
30   For a discussion of the concept of global state, see Ricciardi, 2013.

(Spivak, 1996c: 245) that programmatically limits the possibility of implementing redistributive policies.

Although global, this trend is nevertheless internally differentiated, both because there is a difference between countries in the North and those in the South, where welfare is respectively being dismantled and cannot be established due to restrictions imposed by international financial agencies, and because the absence of social infrastructure has differentiated effects within individual states, affecting mainly migrants, "the diasporic underclass" in the North, and in the South "the rural poor and the urban subproletariat" (Spivak, 1996c: 249). In each of these conditions, women are the ones most intensely affected by domination and exploitation. The emphasis on the difference in their condition, however, should not be taken as the sociologically accurate survey of a situation in which multiple lines of disadvantage intersect. On the contrary, it points to the irreducible difference that makes it necessary to consider the fundamental role of the global state in the reproduction of subalternity *as subalternity* according to the valorization of capital.

The registration of the transformation of the state and its role of political mediation does not imply, for Spivak, the renunciation of confronting "an agenda as impossible as it is necessary" of the battles for "basic civil rights", which remain legitimate aspirations as well as engines of a "real activism", such as that of migrant women and men in metropolitan spaces (Spivak, 1996c: 251–253). However, even the claims for rights – which refer to the now ticklish word emancipation – must take into account the transnational differentiation of the society of capital, of a crisis of the universal in virtue of which every claim is reconfigured in a problematic way on another scene, running the risk of reproducing relations of domination and exploitation. From this point of view, the feminist battles for abortion and sexual freedom made in the 1980s and 1990s take on an exemplary character: by politicizing sexual difference regardless of any consideration of its class determination, the political assertion of a clitoral pleasure released from procreation has effectively ignored the "social practices" that determine sexuality, and with them the specific modes of "ideologico-material repression of the clitoris" that operate within geographically and socially heterogeneous contexts (Spivak, 1987 [1981]: 153). The other side of the celebration of motherhood as a function of increased consumption has been, in "developing" countries, a policy of demographic control managed by national governments with the support of international organizations with the aim of curbing overpopulation, identifying the responsibility "for the exhaustion of the world's resources between the legs of the poorest women in the South" (Spivak 1999: 416). If it is unable to take these differences, these fundamental asymmetries, into account, then feminism risks being co-opted into the circuit of "complicity" between transnational capital and patriarchy (Spivak, 1999: 406), legitimizing subalternity as a condition of possibility, constantly produced and hidden, of emancipation.

Feminism can be transnational to the extent that its "responsibility" towards subaltern women (Spivak, 1996a: 293) allows it to take account of these contradictions, to assume the contestable character of its claims, without however renouncing to make the state, as a "minimal abstract structure" (Butler and Spivak, 2007: 98), the referent of struggles for social justice whose ultimately irrecoverable character allows it to mobilize the claims of subalterns against the capitalist production of subalternity, and thus against the national dimension that – although transformed by global capital – continues to play a decisive role in that production (Spivak, 1996c: 251).[31]

When referred to the subaltern and her experience, the concept of woman therefore affirms a specific polemical and therefore political stance. Not an identity, but a gesture that triggers a "self-separating project" that requires choosing a side (Spivak, 1996 [1993–1994]: 21). By these terms Spivak does not mean a separatist practice animated by a work of self-consciousness, and indeed in some ways overturns radical feminism's slogan "the personal is political", at least to the extent that the latter becomes an exaltation of individualistic biographies incapable of accounting for the way each biography is woven into a history that is not necessarily one's own (Spivak, 2009 [1993]: 4). While Anna Julia Cooper gave voice to the silence of the Black Woman by claiming to be a black woman herself, Spivak is not a subaltern woman, even though she was born in a country marked by colonialism. However, precisely by distancing herself from herself and from her privileged position as an American academic – without denying or repudiating it – she puts herself in the condition of acting as a Gramscian "organic intellectual" (Spivak, 1996a: 292), in order to "listen to" and relate to a voice that is silenced not only by the historical narrative of which "Man" is the sole subject, but also by a feminism incapable of thinking about the social production of sexual difference.

As Spivak's critique of the *Subaltern Studies* group makes clear, this disposition to listen does not seek an antagonistic subaltern "consciousness" or a romanticized "pure" native who, by virtue of her condition, can authentically account for her own subalternity (Spivak, 1996a: 289).[32] On the contrary, in her critique, women can be thought of in the terms in which Marx

---

31   On the problem of "responsibility" see also Spivak, 1994: 19–64.

32   The question of listening recalls the renowned *Can the Subaltern Speak?*, discussed in Morris 2010. For a critique of the category of authenticity in light of sexual difference, see Khanna, 2010: 62–78.

defined *"world-historical,* empirically universal individuals", that is, concretely brought into connection by the global history of society (Marx and Engels 1976 [1845–1846]: 49).[33] Because of the position she occupies in this history – whose narrative has silenced her in order to violently erase the evidence of domination and exploitation – the subaltern woman allows the set of those connections to be brought to light, and continuously poses the problem of the discourse capable of transforming them into a political communication against domination by escaping the logic of its reproduction. The latter, of course, does not concern only sexuality, or the domestic and care work commonly done by women, but the set of hierarchies and forms of oppression that support the global order of exploitation. It is the politicization of its social determination that makes the concept of woman the expression of a global part that demands a stance "for the distant ... horizon of the end of exploitation as such" (Spivak, 1996 [1985a]: n. 5 and 1996a: 296). Something impossible, which one cannot not want.

References

Althusser, L. (1969 [1965]) *For Marx*. London: Penguin.

Althusser, L. and Balibar È. (2016 [1968]) *Reading Capital. The Complete Edition.* New York. Verso.

Anzaldúa, G. (1987) *Borderlands/La Frontera. The New Mestiza.* San Francisco: aunt lute books.

Ardilli, D. (2018) Effetto SCUM. Valerie Solanas e il Femminismo Radicale. In: Arcara S. and Ardilli D. (eds) *Trilogia SCUM. Tutti gli scritti.* Milano: Morellini Editore, 35–60.

Arruzza, C. (2016) Functionalist, Determinist, Reductionist: Social Reproduction Feminism and its Critics. *Science & Society* 1: 9–30.

Atwater, D.F. (1996) (ed) Special issue: The Voices of African American Women in the Civil Rights Movement. *Journal of Black Studies*, 5.

Beauvoir, S. de (1956 [1949]) *The Second Sex*. London: Jonathan Cape.

Bhattacharya, T. (2017) (ed) *Social Reproduction Theory. Remapping Class, Recentering Oppression.* London: Pluto Press.

Bono, P. and Kemp, S. (1991) (eds) *Italian Feminist Thought: A Reader.* London: Blackwell.

Brown, W. (1995) *States of Injury. Power and Freedom in Late Modernity.* Princeton: Princeton University Press.

---

33   Concerning Marx and Engels conception of the "empirically universal" individual, see Ricciardi, 2019: 53.

Brown, W. (2002) Suffering the Paradoxes of Rights. In: Brown W. and Halley J. (eds) *Left Legalism, Left Critique*. Durham: Duke University Press, 420–434.

Butler, J. (1986) Sex and Gender in Simone de Beauvoir's *Second Sex*. *Yale French Studies* 72: 35–49.

Butler, J. (2010 [1990]) *Gender Trouble. Feminism and the Subversion of Identity*. New York – London: Routledge.

Butler, J. and Spivak, G.C. (2007) *Who Sings the Nation State? Language, Politics, Belonging*. London – New York – Calcutta: Seagull.

Cicogna, P. and de Lauretis, T. (1990) (eds) *Sexual Difference: A Theory of Social-Symbolic Practice*. Bloomington: Indiana University Press.

Combahee River Collective (2017 [1977]) *The Combahee River Collective Statement*. In: Taylor, K.Y. (ed) *How We Get Free. Black Feminism and the Combahee River Collective*. Chicago: Haymarket Books, 15–27.

Cooper, M. (2017) *Family Values. Between Neoliberalism and the New Social Conservatism*. New York: Zone Books.

Crenshaw, K. (1989) Demarginalizing the Intersection of Race and Sex: A Black Feminist Critique of Antidiscrimination Doctrine, Feminist Theory and Antiracist Politics. *University of Chicago Legal Forum* 1: 139–167.

Dalla Costa, M. (1974 [1972]) *Potere femminile e sovversione sociale*. Venezia: Marsilio.

Davis, A. (1972) Reflections on the Black Woman's Role in the Community of Slaves. *The Massachusetts Review* 1: 81–100.

Davis, A. (1983 [1981]) *Women, Race and Class*. London: Vintage Books.

De Gouges, O. (1792) Invitation aux dames françaises, pour la fête du maire d'Etampes. In: de Gouges O. (1792), *Lettres à la Reine, aux Généraux de l'Armée, aux Amis de la Constitution, et aux Françaises citoyennes. Description de la fête du 3 juin, par Marie-Olympe de Gouges*. Paris: Société typographique aux Jacobins Saint-Honoré, 11–13.

Del Guadalupe Davidson, M. and Yancy, G. (2009) (ed) *Critical Perspectives on bell hooks*. New York – London: Routledge.

Derrida, J. (1967) *De la Grammatologie*. Paris: Minuit.

Echols, A. (1989) *Daring to Be Bad. Radical Feminism in America 1967–1975*. Minneapolis – London: University of Minnesota Press.

Ellena, L. (2011) Carla Lonzi e il neo-femminismo radicale degli anni '70: disfare la cultura, disfare la politica. In: Conte L., Fiorino V. and Martini V. (eds) *Carla Lonzi: la duplice radicalità. Dalla critica militante al femminismo di Rivolta*. Pisa: ETS, 117–143.

Ferrari, R. (2013) Donne, migrazione, confini. In: Mezzadra S. and Ricciardi M. (eds) *Movimenti indisciplinati. Migrazioni, migranti e discipline scientifiche*. Verona: ombre corte, 29–49.

Fraser, N. (2013) *Fortunes of Feminism. From State-Managed Capitalism to Neoliberal Crisis*. London: Verso books.

Friedan, B. (1970 [1963]) *The Feminine Mystique*. New York: Dell Publishing.

Garbagnoli, S. (2013) Monique Wittig: l'eterosessualità come presupposto. Per una semiologia politica del senso comune. In: Garbagnoli S. and Perilli V. (eds) *Non si nasce donna. Percorsi, testi e contesti del materialismo femminista in Francia.* Roma: Alegre, 143–157.

Gissi, A. (2018) "Le estere". Immigrazione femminile e lavoro domestico in Italia. *Meridiana. Rivista di storia e scienze sociali* 91/1: 37–56.

Guerra, E. (2005) Una nuova soggettività: femminismo e femminismi nel passaggio degli anni Settanta. In: Bertilotti T. and Scattigno A. (eds) *Il femminismo degli anni Settanta.* Roma: Viella, 25–67.

Hall, S. (1996 [1980]) Race, Articulation and Societies Structured in Dominance. In: Baker H.A. Jr., Diawara M. and Lindeborg R.H. (eds) *Black British Cultural Studies: A Reader.* Chicago –London: University of Chicago Press, 14–58.

Hall, S. and Grossberg, L. (1986) On Postmodernism and Articulation: An Interview with Stuart Hall. *Journal of Communication Inquiry* 10: 45–60.

Harris G. (2001) From the Kennedy Commission to the Combahee Collective. Black Feminist Organization, 1960–1980, in Collier B. and Franklin V.P. (eds) *Sisters in the Struggle. African American Women in the Civil Rights – Black Power Movement.* New York: New York University Press, 287–305.

Hegel, G.W.F. (1977 [1807]) *Phenomenology of Spirit.* Miller A.V. and Findlay F.N. (eds). Oxford – New York – Toronto – Melbourne: Oxford University Press.

hooks, b. (1982) *Ain't I a Woman. Black Women and Feminism.* London – Winchester: Pluto Press.

hooks, b. (2000 [1984]) *Feminist Theory. From Margin to Center.* London: Pluto Press.

hooks, b. (2004) *We Real Cool: Black Men and Masculinity.* New York and London: Routledge.

hooks, b. (2009 [2000]) *Where we Stand: Class Matters.* New York and London: Routledge.

hooks, b. (2015 [1990]) *Yearning Race, Gender and Cultural politics.* New York and London: Routledge.

Iamurri, L. (2016) *Un margine che sfugge. Carla Lonzi e l'arte in Italia, 1955–1970.* Macerata: Quodlibet.

Iuliano, F. (2012) *Altri mondi, altre parole. Gayatri Chakravorty Spivak tra decostruzione e impegno militante.* Verona: ombre corte.

Jung, G. (1981 [1934–1954]) *The Collected Works, vol. 9, part I: The Archetypes and the Collective Unconscious.* London: Routledge.

Khanna, R. (2010) On the Name, Ideation and Sexual Difference. *Differences* 2: 62–78.

Koedt, A. (1969) The Myth of the Vaginal Orgasm. Available (consulted 23 April 2023) at: https://www.cwluherstory.org/classic-feminist-writings-articles/myth-of -the-vaginal-orgasm.

Libreria delle donne di Milano (1987) *Non credere di avere dei diritti.* Torino: Rosenberg&Sellier.

Locher-Sholten, E. (2000) *Women and the Colonial State. Essays on Gender and Modernity in the Netherland Indies 1900–1942.* Amsterdam: Amsterdam University Press.

Lonzi, C. (1977 [1971]) La donna clitoridea e la donna vaginale. In: Lonzi C. (1977) *Sputiamo su Hegel. La donna vaginale e la donna clitoridea e altri scritti.* Milano: Scritti di Rivolta femminile, 77–140.

Lonzi, C. (1996 [1970]) Let's Spit on Hegel. In: Jagentowicz Mills P. (ed) *Feminist Interpretations of G.W.F. Hegel.* University Park: Pennsylvania State University Press, 275–297.

Marx, K. (1996 [1867]) *Capital. A Critique of Political Economy*, book 1. In: MECW (1996), vol. 35.

Marx, K. (1998 [1894]) *Capital. A Critique of Political Economy*, book 3. In: MECW (1998), vol. 37.

Marx, K. and Engels, F. (1976 [1845–1846]) *The German Ideology*. In: MECW (1976), vol. 5: 19–539.

Masters, H.W. and Johnson, V.E. (1966) *Human Sexual Response.* Toronto – New York: Bantam Books.

Mies M. (1998 [1986]) *Patriarchy and Accumulation on a World Scale. Women in the International Division of Labor.* London – New York: Zed Books.

Millet, K. (2016 [1969]) *Sexual Politics.* New York: Columbia University Press.

Mohanty, C.T. (2003) *Feminism without Borders. Decolonizing Theory, Practicing Solidarity.* Durham and London: Duke University Press.

Moi, T. (2008 [1999]) *What is a Woman?* Oxford: Oxford University Press.

Moi, T. (2017) *Revolution of the Ordinary. Literary Studies after Wittgenstein, Austin and Cavell.* Chicago: The University of Chicago Press.

Morgan, R. (1970) (ed) *Sisterhood is Powerful. An Anthology of Writings from the Women's Liberation Movement.* New York: Vintage Book.

Morris, R. (2010) (ed) *Can the Subaltern Speak? Reflections on the History of an Idea.* New York: Columbia University Press.

Moynihan, D.P. (1965) *The Negro Family. The Case for National Action.* Office of Policy Planning and Research, United States: Department of Labor.

Picchio. A. and Pincelli, G. (2019) (eds) *Una lotta femminista globale. L'esperienza dei gruppi per il Salario al Lavoro Domestico di Ferrara e Modena.* Milano: FrancoAngeli.

Ramirez, F.O., Soysal, Y. and Shanahan, S. (1997) The Changing Logic of Political Citizenship: Cross-National Acquisition of Women's Suffrage Rights, 1890 to 1990. *American Sociological Review* 5: 735–745.

Redstockings (2018 [1969]) *Redstockings Manifesto.* In: Weiss P.A. and Brueske M. (eds) *Feminist Manifestos. A Global Documentary Reader.* New York: New York University Press, 218–220.

Ricciardi, M. (2013) Dallo Stato moderno allo Stato globale. Storia e trasformazione di un concetto. *Scienza & Politica. Per una storia delle dottrine* 48: 75–93.

Ricciardi, M. (2017) Appunti per una teoria politica delle migrazioni: potere sociale e politicizzazione della differenza. In: Chignola S. and Sacchetto D. (eds) *Le reti del valore. Migrazioni, produzione e il governo della crisi*. Roma: DeriveApprodi, 108–124.

Ricciardi, M. (2019) *Il potere temporaneo. Karl Marx e la politica come critica della società*. Milano: Meltemi.

Rivolta femminile (1977 [1971]) Sessualità femminile e aborto. In: Lonzi C. (1977) *Sputiamo su Hegel. La donna vaginale e la donna clitoridea e altri scritti*. Milano: Scritti di Rivolta femminile, 67–75.

Rivolta femminile (2018 [1970]) Female Revolt Manifesto. In: Weiss P.A. and Brueske M. (eds) *Feminist Manifestos. A Global Documentary Reader*. New York: New York University Press, 226–230.

Roth, B. (2004) *Separated Roads to Feminism. Black, Chicana and White Feminist Movements in America's Second Wave*. Cambridge: Cambridge University Press.

Rudan, P. (2019) Il femminismo e Marx. Sull'orlo di una frattura. *Filosofia Politica* 2: 267–284.

Rudan, P. (2020a) Omologazione, differenza, rivolta. Carla Lonzi e l'imprevisto dell'ordine patriarcale. In: Baritono R. and Ricciardi M. (eds) *Strategie dell'ordine: categorie, fratture, soggetti*. Bologna: "Quaderni di Scienza & Politica" 8, 261–282.

Rudan, P. (2020b) Gayatri Spivak e il femminismo come critica globale. In: Mellino M. and Ruben Pomella A. (eds) *Marx nei margini. Dal marxismo nero al femminismo postcoloniale*. Roma: Alegre, 115–134.

Southard, B. (1993) Colonial Politics and Women's Rights. Woman Suffrage Campaigns in Bengal, British India, in the 1920. *Modern Asian Studies* 27(2): 397–493.

Spivak, G.C. (1987 [1981]) French Feminism in an International Frame. In: Spivak G.C. *In Other Words. Essays in Cultural Politics*. New York and London: Methuen, 134–153.

Spivak, G.C. (1994) Responsibility. *Boundary* 3: 19–64.

Spivak, G.C. (1996 [1985a]) Scattered Speculations on the Question of Value. In: Landry D. and MacLean G. (eds) *The Spivak Reader*. New York – London: Routledge, 107–140.

Spivak, G.C. (1996 [1985b]) Feminism and Critical Theory. In: Landry D. and MacLean G.(eds) *The Spivak Reader*. New York – London: Routledge, 53–74.

Spivak, G.C. (1996 [1985c]) Subaltern Studies. Deconstructing Historiography. In: Landry D. and MacLean G. (eds) *The Spivak Reader*. New York – London: Routledge, 203–235.

Spivak, G.C. (1996 [1993–1994]) Bonding in Difference. Interview with Alfred Arteaga. In: Landry D. and MacLean G. (eds) *The Spivak Reader*. New York – London: Routledge, 15–28.

Spivak, G.C. (1996a) Subaltern Talk. Interview with the Editors. In: Landry D. and MacLean, G. (eds) *The Spivak Reader*. New York – London: Routledge, 287–308.

Spivak, G.C. (1996b) "Woman" as Theatre. United Nations Conference on Women, Beijing 1995. *Radical Philosophy* 75: 2–4.

Spivak, G.C. (1996c) Diasporas Old and New: Women in the Transnational World. *Textual Practice* 2: 245–269.

Spivak, G.C. (1999) *A Critique of Postcolonial Reason. Toward a History of the Vanishing Present.* Cambridge (MS) – London: Harvard University Press.

Spivak, G.C. (2009 [1993]) *Outside in the Teaching Machine.* New York: Routledge.

Taylor, K.Y. (2017) Introduction. In: Taylor K.Y. (ed) *How We Get Free. Black Feminism and the Combahee River Collective.* Chicago: Haymarket Books, 1–14.

Thébaud F. (1992) (ed) *Storia delle donne. Il Novecento.* Roma – Bari: Laterza.

United Nation (1985) The Nairobi Forward-Looking Strategies for the Advancement of Women. Available (consulted 23 April 2023) at: https://1997-2001.state.gov/picw/archives/nairobi-contents.html.

Weeks, K. (2011) *The Problem of Work.* Durham – London: Duke University Press.

Wittig, M. (1992 [1980–1989]) *The Straight Mind.* Boston (MS): Beacon Press.

Zapperi, G. (2017) *Carla Lonzi. Un'arte della vita.* Roma: DeriveApprodi.

Zappino, F. (2019) La distruzione dell'eterosessualità. In: Wittig, M. *Il pensiero eterosessuale.* Verona: ombre corte, 122–143.

Index